DAILY HABIT EVOLUTION

17 SMALL CHANGES TO CONQUER DISTRACTIONS AND MASTER TIME MANAGEMENT

THE POSITIVITY POLICY

© **Copyright 2021 - All rights reserved.**

The content contained within this book may not be reproduced, duplicated or transmitted without direct written permission from the author or the publisher.

Under no circumstances will any blame or legal responsibility be held against the publisher, or author, for any damages, reparation, or monetary loss due to the information contained within this book, either directly or indirectly.

Legal Notice:

This book is copyright protected. It is only for personal use. You cannot amend, distribute, sell, use, quote or paraphrase any part, or the content within this book, without the consent of the author or publisher.

Disclaimer Notice:

Please note the information contained within this document is for educational and entertainment purposes only. All effort has been executed to present accurate, up to date, reliable, complete information. No warranties of any kind are declared or implied. Readers acknowledge that the author is not engaged in the rendering of legal, financial, medical or professional advice. The content within this book has been derived from various sources. Please consult a licensed professional before attempting any techniques outlined in this book.

By reading this document, the reader agrees that under no circumstances is the author responsible for any losses, direct or indirect, that are incurred as a result of the use of the information contained within this document, including, but not limited to, errors, omissions, or inaccuracies.

CONTENTS

Introduction   7

1. MINOR MORNING MODIFICATIONS   11
   Habit 1: Get an Early Start   11
   Habit 2: Prioritize Your Mind and Body   20
   Habit 3: Preview Your Day   25
   Habit 4: Get Your Blood Pumping   26

2. WHAT IS WEALTH?   29
   The Value of Your Time   31
   What Is Your Time Worth?   32
   The Importance of Making the Most of Your Time   36

3. DAILY DISCIPLINES   42
   Habit 5: Always Carry a Notebook   43
   Habit 6: Identify the "MIT" and Always Prioritize It   46
   Habit 7: Be Your Own Parent—Limit Your Screen Time   48
   Habit 8: Only Touch It Once   53
   Habit 9: If It Takes Less Than Two Minutes, Do It Now   55
   Habit 10: Goal-Driven Actions   58
   Habit 11: Don't Overcomplicate Things   62

4. CONSTANT CONTROL VS. CONSTANT CHANGE   69
   What Is Time Blocking?   69
   The Benefits of Time Blocking   74

5. EMBRACE THE END (OF YOUR DAY) — 79
   Habit 12: Calm Your Mind as There Is Always More to Do — 80
   Habit 13: Plan Meals Ahead — 84
   Habit 14: Have Some Time to Unwind — 87
   Habit 15: Plan Your Next Day — 93
   Habit 16: Power of Positivity — 95
   Habit 17: Put Your Phone Away — 101

6. GETTING TIME TAKES TIME — 105
   Changing Your Bad Habits — 106
   Tips for Making Your Habits Stick — 109

Conclusion — 123
Leave a Review — 127
References — 129
About the Authors — 137

WWW.POSITIVITYPOLICY.INFO

FREE GIFT FOR OUR READERS

Get a jump on eliminating negative habits and building your confidence with this checklist. Visit the link:

www.PositivityPolicy.info

INTRODUCTION

Do you want to be more productive and create more time in your day? Of course, you do! Every person wants this. Time is one of our most essential resources, and it is something that is so limited. Think about it; once it's gone, we can't make more of it. This means that we have to use the time we have wisely. The way we use our time will determine how far we get in life and whether or not we are satisfied with the life we live. This is a vital resource to steward well.

The problem is that most people don't know how to use their time in a way that benefits them. We hear people talk about how tasks are a waste of time or how procrastination gets the better of them. There are very few people who actually know how to manage their time well. Unfortunately, this is not a skill that is taught in school or even in university. The topic seems glossed over, and we have to figure it out for ourselves.

INTRODUCTION

There have probably been quite a few days where you were so busy at work, but t didn't feel like you made any progress when your day ended. This can make you feel like you are drowning in a pool of your responsibilities. Your days just run away from you, and you end up working late hours trying to catch up. This leads to feelings of inadequacy and being completely overwhelmed. This is not a great space to be in, but most people just accept that this is their life. We can tell you right now that this is not how it is supposed to be.

A well-balanced life is actually attainable. Living in a balanced way allows you to be productive in a definitive amount of time so that work doesn't have to spill over into other areas of your life. Distractions, poor time management, and bad habits are keeping you from being your most productive self. If you want to move into that space of maximum productivity and success, you need to address these issues in the proper manner.

Imagine waking up full of energy and carrying that throughout your day, being able to walk into work with a purpose for your day, and meet the goals that you set for yourself. Then, once you end your workday, you could use that time the way you want to because you aren't worried about work that didn't get done. Lastly, when you put your head on your pillow, imagine that you could fall into a restful sleep that will fuel you for the day to come. This is not a wishful scenario but something that is entirely possible if the right habits are implemented.

INTRODUCTION

Our habits dictate how our day will go, and at the end, where our lives will lead us. The reason for this is that habits are the things we do almost unconsciously. Our brain creates pathways to make things that we continuously do happen without much effort from us. If we choose to make these habits things that will work to our benefit, we will end up being more productive while needing less intentional effort from our side. It will be almost like a default setting. This book is going to go in-depth on the best habits that will help you get these results if you truly embrace them as your default ones.

We are the Positivity Policy, made up of Kara and Denny, and together we have gone through a lot in life that has put us on the right path to creating habits that reward us with time. We are incredibly passionate about valuing time and using it in the best way possible. Life is all about experiences and having adventures together. Using habits in the right way can lead you to live a life filled with experiences that you cherish today and fond memories that you'll be able to reflect on tomorrow.

We believe that time is the most valuable form of currency. You can use it to increase your standard of living and create the life that you desire. After studying habits for over a decade and trying out many different strategies, we have come up with the 17 best habits that every person should know in order to use their time better and build a life that is a reflection of them.

It took us a while to get to the place we are in because we had to learn it all ourselves. We don't want that for you. We want you

INTRODUCTION

to be empowered to step into this as quickly as possible. The earlier you internalize the principles and build these habits into your life, the sooner you can start living a life that is less stressful and more productive. Time wasted on things that are not important is time that you can't get back. Diving into this requires you to be focused on earning time so that you are able to do the things that really matter to you. We have been through this journey, and now it is time to share our knowledge with you so that you can better manage your time and energy.

By the time you finish this book, you will be well-equipped to live your most productive life. You will begin to uncover the bad habits in your life by comparing them to these 17 habits that lead to saving time and living an overall better life. The habits are laid out in a way that shows you the best structure for your day. You will see habits that apply to every part of your day. We will also be going through other tips and tricks that will help you implement these habits most easily without getting completely overwhelmed. We want you to be fully equipped with the tools you need when you come to the end of this book.

If you are ready to turn your life around and create a life that has space for all the essential things in your life, then you have come to the right place. We will start by talking about your ideal morning. So let's jump right in.

1

MINOR MORNING MODIFICATIONS

The way your mornings go will be a direct reflection on how the rest of your day will go. Starting your morning right will give you the right mindset and energy to get through the rest of your day in the best way possible.

HABIT 1: GET AN EARLY START

If you do some research into the routines of insanely successful people, you will see that there is a common thread that links them. This thread is waking up early. We know for some of you it may feel like the absolute worst suggestion, but try and keep an open mind. It's not a coincidence that people who achieve similar results and successes share habits, so let's try and learn from their behaviors and use these lessons to our benefit.

How you start off your mornings will dictate how the rest of your day will go. People who wake up earlier have been shown to be more productive, get better grades, are more likely to stick to a diet plan, and are healthier in general. There are a lot of benefits to just waking up a bit earlier. The truth is that waking up earlier gives you more time and allows you to accomplish your goals.

Tim Cook, Apple's CEO, wakes up at 3:45 a.m. CEO of General Motors, Mary Barra, wakes up between 4:00 a.m. and 5:00 a.m. Indra Nooyi, CEO of PepsiCo, wakes up by 4:00 a.m. Richard Branson, CEO of the Virgin Group, wakes up before 5:45 a.m. These are just some of the examples of successful people that have made waking up early a priority in their lives. There are some variations in the time that each one wakes up, so you also have the freedom to pick a time that works best for you. Generally, waking up between 5:00 a.m. and 6:00 a.m. is a good time for most people.

These successful people have chosen to wake up early to reap the myriad of benefits it brings. The human body does not just wake up, ready for the day. You need to give it time to wake up properly and get over sleep inertia. It can take over two hours for your body to reach a state of being fully awake. So if you are the type of person who wakes up half an hour before they have to be at work, this is more than likely making your mornings very unproductive, even if you feel like you might have mastered that rushed 30 minutes. When you get to your desk, you won't be able to concentrate correctly or perform at an optimal level because you are trying to fight against the natural fatigue and brain fog that happens when you wake up.

People who wake up earlier are often more positive and have more energy. We know this seems counterintuitive to wake up earlier and have more energy, but it really works. We're not saying to lose sleep by continuing going to bed as late as we usually do, but rather shift things back when it comes to your sleep schedule. Go to bed a bit earlier, and wake up and start your day earlier. You might find that it takes your body a while to get used to waking up earlier, but once you have become accustomed to it, you will see an improvement in your mood, energy levels, and overall productivity. Having a more positive attitude will also help you get a better quality of sleep. There are so many people that struggle to fall asleep at night because their minds are filled with harmful and anxious thoughts.

Speaking of sleep quality, people who wake up earlier also end up sleeping longer than night owls who wake up later. When you choose to wake up earlier, you are also tired much earlier, so you fall asleep quicker when you go to bed. There is less of a chance of rolling around trying to fall asleep. This helps you feel well-rested when you get up the following day. You will have a solid night's sleep that will give you the energy for the day ahead.

When you wake up early, you have more time than other people do. You can get moving and accomplish things earlier, and your day will be more productive. You can get the most important things out of the way before the rest of the world wakes up. This means that you will be far ahead of your peers. Earlier risers tend to advance in the workforce much quicker than their counterparts due to all of these reasons we have just discussed.

If you are someone who has woken up late all your life, you will probably find it hard to switch over to waking up earlier. This is to be expected, but there are some things that you can do to make it easier for yourself. If you incorporate these tips into your mornings and planning, you will find that waking up earlier isn't as complicated as you might initially think. Before you know it, you'll have this incredibly beneficial habit on cruise control.

Ease Into It

It will be challenging for you to start waking up at 5:00 a.m. if you have been waking up after 7:00 a.m. for the past few years. The best way to go about changing this habit is to start slow. Instead of setting your alarm for two hours earlier, try 15 minutes earlier. Do this for a few days, and then add another 15 minutes so that you are waking up 30 minutes earlier than usual. Continue this pattern until you are able to wake up at your desired time.

This will give your body the chance to get used to waking up a bit earlier. You will definitely be tired if you just jump into it. This is the reason many people give up on waking up earlier. They think that they are just not suited for it, but they just went about it the wrong way. Our bodies need time to acclimate to pretty much any physical change, and sleep is definitely not an exception to this.

Go to Bed at a Decent Time

You will definitely be tired in the morning if you do not go to bed early enough. You still need to get seven to eight hours of sleep each night. When your wake-up time shifts, so will your going-to-bed time.

When you first try to go to bed earlier, you will probably struggle to fall asleep. Try and do things that will relax you and allow you to fall asleep quite quickly. One of the best tips is to ensure that you are not staring into any devices that emit blue light. These include cell phones, tablets, TVs, and computers. The light from these devices tricks your body into thinking that it is still daytime, and so you stay awake for longer. Putting all of these devices away at least 30 minutes before you jump into bed will help you fall asleep much easier.

Try making a bedtime routine so that your body will recognize when it is time to wind down. Taking a shower or bath, writing in your journal, planning your tasks for the next day, taking out your clothes for the morning, and reading a book are all great nighttime activities. They are relaxing and help you to clear your mind. Adding a few of these things to your routine will see to it that you fall asleep quicker and have a better quality of sleep overall.

Place Your Phone or Alarm on the Other Side of the Room

Most of us need something to wake us up in the morning, which is why an alarm comes in handy. However, pressing that snooze button is all too easy when your phone or alarm clock is right next to you. To prevent this, place your alarm on the other side of the room. When it rings, you will have to get out of bed and walk over to the alarm to switch it off. Since you are already out of bed, you can just continue with your morning and not be tempted to curl under the blankets for another ten minutes of sleep. If you use a voice activated alarm, such as an Amazon or Google device, you may want to change this up until your discipline levels exceed your temptation to say "Alexa, snooze." This will be an acceptable option to incorporate back into your life once this habit is second nature.

In any case, that extra few minutes of sleep that you get when you snooze your alarm makes you more tired. Once your sleep breaks, you need a good 30 to 60 minutes to get back into a deep sleep that will help you feel rested. The short naps in between alarms are really not doing anything for you.

Once your body is used to waking up at a specific time, you might be able to skip the alarm altogether. Your body will just wake up naturally in the morning. You will feel much better and have more energy when you wake up naturally. Your body clock should adjust itself to the new routine within a few weeks. If you need to continue with the alarm, then you can do that as well.

Reward Yourself for Waking Up Early

Many people think that waking up early is a punishment. When we have this mindset, it makes it hard to motivate ourselves to get out of bed in the morning. The list of things you need to get done is also not a good motivator. When you wake up, give yourself something to look forward to, and you will find that hopping out of bed is a much easier task.

These motivators don't have to be big things; they just have to be something you can look forward to. You could reward yourself with a stop at your favorite coffee shop. If you enjoy meditation and journaling, you can give yourself time to do this in the morning. Some people really love going for a walk or to the gym when they wake up. Even just something small like listening to part of that podcast, catching your favorite morning radio show, playing with your dog or cat, and having an overall sense of control of your morning instead of being rushed can work well to make a huge difference. You need to find what motivates you to get out of bed. Once you start doing these things and have something to look forward to rather than dreading that morning scramble to get ready quickly, so you don't end up being late, you will see that getting out of bed becomes more of a joy than a chore.

Have a Plan for Your Mornings

Now that you are waking up earlier, you need to know what you will do during that time. It is no use waking up early and then sitting on your couch until it is time to leave for work. Having a morning routine will help you to be productive and get things done during this time.

You don't necessarily have to start work earlier when you wake up earlier. You can use it as a time to do things you wouldn't have time for after work. Working on a passion project or side hustle can be done in the mornings if you find that you are too tired to do so when you get home from work. Meal prepping for the day is also a good option. Yoga, meditation, and exercise are things we tend to leave on the back burner when we have hectic days, so prioritizing them in the morning is the best way to make sure they all get done. You could also take some time to work on a hobby and do something for yourself. This will put you in a good mood for the rest of the day.

Be Consistent

Once you have decided that you will wake up earlier, you have to be consistent with it. This includes waking up early on the weekends. Our bodies work on routine. You will find that you get hungry, tired, feel energetic, and wake up all around the same time each day. Once our body finds a rhythm, it wants to stick to it. Your body doesn't have internal programming that makes it respond differently on weekends or Holidays. It's essential to mentally acknowledge this, so we don't try to set up a weekday habit and a weekend habit because the constant change will make it quite tricky to solidify this habit. This isn't to say that you can't sleep in on occasion when you celebrate something and happen to stay up later than usual, but just don't make breaking your success habits something regular or routine.

If you are getting enough sleep every single night, then you won't have that temptation to sleep in on the weekends anyway. Your weekends can and really should be productive parts of your life even if you aren't working. You will find that you can get a whole lot more out of your weekends when you wake up earlier. If you feel like you need some extra sleep, you can go to bed earlier at night. However, the truth is that you can't actually catch up on sleep. So trying to squeeze in some extra shut-eye on the weekends doesn't actually work in the ways you may think; we aren't batteries that can be on the charger today to make up for the extra juice we spent yesterday.

Consistency is key with everything in life. Try your best to keep it consistent every single day. You will find that you won't struggle to keep this habit of waking up earlier during the week if you kept to your sleep schedule on the weekends.

HABIT 2: PRIORITIZE YOUR MIND AND BODY

For most of us, the first thing we do in the morning is reach over and check our phones. It is almost like a reflex. We quickly browse through our emails, check the news, and scroll through Facebook, Twitter, Instagram, and TikTok. While this may seem like a pretty harmless activity, it actually comes with some pretty astoundingly negative consequences. The first hour of your day should be dedicated to your mind and body, not your phone and emails.

When you check your phone while you are still in bed, your morning routine is pretty much ruined before it even begins. All the things that you planned on doing become much more challenging because you have distracted yourself with other things. While you may not start replying to the work emails when you first see them, your mind will be consumed with the thought of them. It will make it much more challenging to do other things because your mind will be pulled back to your messages and emails.

When you see the list of notifications and messages that have come through during the night, you have given yourself a to-do list before you have even woken up. These things feel like urgent things, and they can distract you from what you are actually supposed to be doing. The morning is supposed to be a time of calm and relaxation before you step into the business of the day. Your phone doesn't make good company if you are trying to feel calm in the morning.

Studies have shown that people who check their phones when they wake up have higher stress levels, feel more discontent throughout the day, and have higher anxiety levels. Let's break these three things down and see how checking your phone in the morning results in these feelings.

Higher stress levels are caused by feeling like you have many things to do and not enough time to do them. It comes from being overwhelmed and overstimulated. Notifications always feel important, even when they are just someone saying hi. We feel as though we are obligated to check them and respond. So when you see a whole bunch of notifications from the night before, you feel obligated to go through each one. This long list of things creates a stressed feeling because you have so many different things to think about and respond to before your body has woken up properly. You will end up carrying this feeling of stress throughout the day. Plus, you will be more likely to keep checking your notifications throughout the day because that is how you started your day. This leads to you constantly being interrupted when you are doing other important tasks, which again leads to more stress.

Checking your phone in the morning can cause you to compare yourself to others or feel like you are missing out on something. If this is how you start your day, then it will be very difficult to shake that feeling as the day progresses. Social media makes us look at all the amazing things other people have and are doing. Then, looking at our own lives, it can appear to pale in comparison. The problem here is that people are only posting the good things, and you don't get a proper representation of their lives. Every person has negatives in their lives because not a single person is perfect. Comparing your average daily to someone else's highlights is the quickest way to discontentment and the feeling that you are not doing enough. It can easily make you feel inadequate, which will make you less productive, and you will be unhappy throughout the day.

Lastly is the feeling of anxiety. When we are under pressure, we can associate notifications and emails with something negative. Perhaps something new is being added to our plate, or the boss is unhappy with the work we did. Simply hearing the notification tone or seeing it pop up on the screen allows anxiety to bubble up within you. Starting your day feeling anxious thoughts is not the best. You will find it hard to concentrate on the things you are doing because you will be thinking about the things in your emails and other notifications. The only way to prevent this is to allocate specific times to check your messages and notifications, and this time should not be in the morning. Blocking off specific times to check your phone and emails, especially those tied to a job, can lower anxiety by a large degree. You won't be able to hear the notification sound, so you will not know when you get a message. This will also help you to remain present and focused on what you are doing. Even if you are just doing yoga, reading, or having your morning cup of coffee, you shouldn't be worried about the messages coming in. Being present in the moment helps you to lower levels of stress and anxiety because it clears your mind and puts you in control of your thoughts.

With all of this being said, it leaves the question of what you should be doing first thing in the morning. The first hour of your day should be focused on your mental and physical health. This can include anything that you think would benefit these two areas. When you first get up in the morning, you need to give your mind and body the chance to wake up fully, as we stated earlier on.

Exercise is a fantastic habit to include in your morning routine. You will reap the benefits of this throughout the day. Exercise actually increases your energy levels, and this increase will stick with you throughout the entire day. So, even if it takes a little push to get going, you'll find it's easier to keep moving once you get moving, and this exercise will increase your daily productivity. This doesn't have to be anything hectic; just a morning walk or jog will yield benefits. Your willpower is higher earlier in the day, so it is easier to convince yourself to exercise in the morning. You can easily get carried away with the day and then skip the workout if you leave it for the end of the day. Plus you are often too tired when you get home from work, so you don't want to exercise. We will speak more about this later on in this chapter.

When it comes to your mind, you have a lot of options. Journaling, meditation, reading, and doing something you love can all be great options for you. Meditation will help you clear your mind to start off your day in a calm state. Journaling enables you to vent your negative thoughts, save your grand ideas, or even just pour out all of the thoughts floating around in your head to improve the clarity of your mind. Once they are out of your mind and on paper, you will think about them less. This means there is less chance of you being distracted by these things when you are supposed to be focusing on something else. Reading and doing something you love is a form of bettering yourself and learning. You are learning something or increasing one of your skill sets. This will make you feel a sense of pride, knowing you've been productive even before you start work. Talk about a great feeling to carry into your workday.

The way you implement these two things is really up to you. The important thing is that you make space for them in your morning. You will see positive differences in yourself and your productivity levels when you commit to doing some of these things every morning. It may be difficult in the beginning, but after a few weeks, it will become a habit, and before you know it, every morning, you will wake up looking forward to spending this valuable time on yourself.

HABIT 3: PREVIEW YOUR DAY

Your mornings are a setup for the rest of the day. If you are unorganized, stressed, and rushed in the morning, this is a reflection of what the rest of your day is going to look like. A great habit to pick up in the morning is to plan your day. It will help set you up, and you will have a clear goal and know where you are headed. Most people who fail to have productive days just do the work that pops up in front of them. This means that they are never really intentionally working towards any goals and are just doing the tasks that seem important at the moment but don't really yield any results. If you're still getting in the habit of getting up earlier, don't worry! Just add this habit to the night before. Preview tomorrow before you go to bed, so you wake up with a game plan. Eventually, when you have enough time in the morning by getting up earlier, you can shift that time spent from the night before to the morning of, or maybe a combination of the two.

One of the biggest mistakes you can make when planning out your day is giving yourself too much to do. As much as we would all like to think that we can accomplish a whole lot of things in a day, it is simply not true. You should give yourself one to three big goals for the day, and then all your tasks can revolve around those goals. This is manageable, and you can see the progress as you complete the tasks you need to. If you put too much on your plate, you will feel demotivated at the end of the day if you are unable to complete all the tasks you have set out for yourself. You don't want to end your day off on a low note.

When you are setting up your list of goals, make sure you are aware of their priority. Important things should be given the most attention and should be done first. The less important things can be handled later on in the day when you don't need to be as focused. Naturally, we all get tired and concentrate less as the day goes on. This is why you need to accomplish the most important tasks first. If you are unable to complete the rest of the things on your list for some reason, you will know that the highest priority tasks are complete, and that alone will give you some positive momentum toward your productivity in the days to come. Getting derailed when it comes to vital tasks is what will set you back. The things of lesser importance can, and should, be shuffled around a bit more.

These are just the basics of getting your day in order. There is a lot more to dive into when it comes to this topic, as it is something that will really set you up for success. Everyone wants to be able to reach their goals, and it isn't a complicated process if you know what you are doing.

HABIT 4: GET YOUR BLOOD PUMPING

Thirty minutes is the recommended amount of exercise a person should be getting in each day. When you think about it, it's not really that much. However, many people still struggle to meet that goal because of busy schedules and other commitments. Getting in your exercise in the morning is the best way to make sure you work out and reap all the benefits that come with it.

Exercising in the morning gives you a goal to achieve first thing when you wake up. This means that you have something to motivate you not to hit that snooze button. You know you need to get up and exercise; otherwise, you won't be able to do it later, and there is only a specific amount of time you have in the morning to get it done. Committing to this practice helps you to establish a solid morning routine.

Once you have done your workout for the day, you will find that you have even more energy than that cup of coffee in the morning rewards you with. This energy boost is not something that is short-lived; instead, it lasts throughout the whole day. You will also find that your mind will be clearer, and you will be in a better mood. All of this results from the chemical processes that happen in your brain and body when you exercise. We were not meant to just sit around all day. Our bodies were made for movement. The more you move and challenge your body, the better you will feel.

If you struggle with maintaining a healthy diet, then exercising in the morning could be part of the solution to this problem, too. Starting your day off with something healthy will make you more likely to continue with the healthy trend throughout the day. As humans, we tend to try just as hard not to lose progress as we do to actually make it. This helps build this habit, as it will internally drive you not to ruin the effort you put into your exercise by making poor dietary choices throughout the day.

2

WHAT IS WEALTH?

The first four habits you've learned about are some that will have an immediate impact on your daily routine, and in turn, your everyday life. Every one of the seventeen habits has an underlying purpose, which is to maximize your time management skills and productivity through each of your days, so before jumping into the rest of them, we think it's essential to get a firm grasp on what time is and how it relates to our lives.

Most of us are guilty of having been taught that our wealth is determined by the amount of money we have in the bank. Because of this, we spend all our time working to on getting more money. In turn, most people never really get to do the things they love or desire to do because they are so busy trying to accumulate this wealth in the hopes of one day being able to enjoy it. A lucky few make it to the point where they have saved up enough to enjoy the last few years of their lives doing something they have always wanted to do.

We don't know about you, but that all sounds incredibly depressing to us. Working so hard your whole life to accumulate enough money in the hopes of being financially free when you are in your 60s or 70s doesn't actually sound like a life someone would wish for themselves. Yet, so many people get caught up in this model of living. It is what we know, so we tend to stick to it.

When the details are laid before us, it's easy to see that the reason we get caught up in this money-focused road to wealth is that we actually don't know what wealth is or how to get it. Money may be part of wealth, but it certainly is not all of it. When you are on a journey to accumulate wealth within your life, you should ask yourself why you want it. Most of the time, the answer would be that being financially free means you can spend your time doing what you really want to do. This may be working on a passion project, traveling, or simply spending more time with your loved ones. If we are completely honest with ourselves, it's more time we are seeking rather than money.

We work so hard to get ahead financially because we think that money buys us more time, but in fact, it is the other way around. As much as it would be nice to have fancy items, they are not the things that will bring you internal happiness. Freedom brings happiness, and it is the thing that most people desire. Truthfully, all of us want that very freedom to spend our time doing what we enjoy most.

Now taking all of this into consideration, we can see that the most valuable thing in life is time. Time is not only what we all strive to have more of, but it almost always directly correlates with how much money we can make. True wealth is therefore defined by time because it holds more value than money. The problem is that most people don't know how to use time in their favor, and that is why they spend so many hours working in the hopes of one day being free.

THE VALUE OF YOUR TIME

Simply put, every single person has the same amount of time in the day. At the start of life, we are all given an indefinite amount of time to make something of ourselves, so although we all model our lives around a certain amount of years, nothing is promised. Not all uses of time are equal, either. This is why some people end up creating a ton of wealth for themselves in a short amount of years, and others never seem to get themselves off the ground regardless of how many years they work.

Naturally, someone who spends their time doing work that generates a lot of money will have more money than someone who works for minimum wage, even if they work the same number of hours. The same principle will be true in every area of life. If you spend your time building deep relationships, you will have long-lasting friendships. However, if you use your time to hop from one social circle to the next, you won't have any relationships with solid foundations. A person who focuses their time on tasks that will help their community and less fortunate people will have more impact on those around them than someone who stays home on the weekends, where you spend your time matters.

We use the same terms when we talk about time as we do when we talk about money, as both will be spent based on our choosing. We waste time, and we waste money. We can also save time and save money. Money is exchanged for something that we actually want or need. Time is supposed to be used in the same manner. We are meant to use time as a tool to get the things that we really want. It is often not thought of like this, and that is where many people make a mistake. If you want a stronger relationship, you will need to trade in some time to work on it. If you want more money, you will need to trade in time to put in more work to make more money. This works for everything in life, and it leads us to the truth that time is our most important resource. Whether it is indirectly or directly, you will need to trade time for everything in life.

WHAT IS YOUR TIME WORTH?

To use your time effectively to build wealth and be financially free, you need to figure out how much your time is worth. Before you do this, you must understand that there is a trade-off between time and money. How much your time is worth is determined by how much money you would spend to save a certain amount of time.

For example, if you were looking to buy a new bookcase, your options are to buy one online and hire someone to build it for you or go to the store and pick it up and build it yourself. Let's say the bookcase is $80 and delivery and installation another $40. If you were to go to the store to fetch the bookcase and build it yourself, you would probably be giving up a solid three to four hours of your time but saving $40. What you choose to do will determine the amount of value you think your time has. If you decide to do it yourself, you believe that your time is worth less than $10 per hour since that is what you will be saving. Inherently we all know how valuable our time is to us. That is why, when you read the first half of this paragraph, you already knew what you were going to do.

Most CEOs of a large company will always choose to spend money to save time. This is because they know the value their time holds. They would lose more money by fetching and building the bookcase than by just paying someone else to do it for them. This is why people who hold high-level positions hire people to do menial tasks like picking up laundry, walking the dog, cooking, and cleaning the house. These things all take time, but they do not make money. If a CEO chose to do these things instead of work, they would lose the company some big bucks. On the other hand, someone who works for minimum wage might not be willing to pay someone to deliver and build the bookcase for them because their time is worth less in terms of dollars per hour. If the minimum wage worker were to construct the bookcase themselves, they would save money because working those extra hours isn't going to compensate for the additional cost of the delivery and builder. While we all have the same amount of time in the day, the value of that time depends on how we spend it.

Don't misread that paragraph, as we're not suggesting that everyone just hires people to do everything for them in life. It's merely to illustrate a point. This principle does not only apply when you want to trade your time so that you can make more money. People trade their money so that they can have more free time as well. You can pay someone to mow the lawn or clean the pool so that you have more time to relax on the weekends. Whatever you choose to do determines how much value you place on time versus money.

We unconsciously make these kinds of choices every single day. The trick is to notice when you are doing it so that you can train yourself to make the choices that will be of the most benefit to you. Saying no to working on the weekends on a project for your boss will free you up to use that same time to work on a business idea that could yield more benefits to you in the future. Every single decision that involves using your time should be weighed like this so that you are able to make the best choices.

You can figure out how much an hour is worth to you by knowing the amount of money you could be making in an hour. You will need different figures to work this out. First, you need to know how many hours you work in a year. For most people who work a nine-to-five job and commute to work, this would be about 2,500 hours a year (Clear, n.d.). You need to account for all the time spent working on work-related things, including commuting, coming home, finishing up a project, taking after-hours calls, and attending meetings. These will add up, so make sure you are taking these into account because this time is not being used to do anything else productive. You might need to be intentional about tracking your time for a month or two so that you can get an accurate number.

Once you have the number of hours you work per year, you will need to take your yearly salary and divide it by that number. If you earn $40,000 per year, you will divide it by 2,500 hours, which works out to $16.00 per hour. That is how much each of your hours is worth. In this case, it could be an excellent option for you to pay for someone to deliver and build your bookcase rather than you doing it yourself because you would be losing $16.00 for every hour you spend doing that task. If you are unhappy with the value of your time, then it is up to you to take a chance and find something that will give you more monetary reward for the time put in. This is why people say you should work smarter, not harder.

THE IMPORTANCE OF MAKING THE MOST OF YOUR TIME

It is up to you to choose what to do with your time. Your decisions will directly affect how your life will turn out and how successful you will be. Time is the only resource that can be traded in for such a big reward or be wasted in a way that prevents you from reaching your full potential. Time is something that has enormous significance in the life of every person.

The More Time You Have, the More Wealth You Can Build

Financial freedom works in years, not dollars. This means that the more time you have, the higher your chance of reaching financial freedom. The reason behind this is that a dollar saved is worth more than a dollar earned (Roth, 2011). The longer you have money in an investment, the more it will be worth over time. It increases through compounding interest, and at the end of the day, it gives you back more than what you put in.

If you were to get a promotion and earn $5,000 extra per year, some of that would go to taxes, and you would definitely be tempted to increase your standard of living by a small degree. However, if you were to place $5,000 in your savings and choose to spend less throughout the year, you would have three times as much money in your savings than had you just kept increasing the amount of money you earned. Saving money is a much better strategy than making more money. In many cases, earning more money requires you to put in more work and time in order to do so. Saving money requires no time or effort from you, other than fighting those nagging temptations to spend more because you "earned it." A great goal is to save money and let it grow for the most extended amount of time. This practice is part of a winning strategy for financial freedom.

There are many people who work towards financial freedom. The younger they start saving towards that goal, the more money they can accumulate. The longer you wait to start saving, the more money you will need to save in order to reach the amount you need to be financially free. This is why how long your money will be invested is more important than the initial amount you place in the investment.

You Don't Know How Much You Have Left

At the end of the day, we don't know how much time we have left. We can give it our best guess, but we will never know until we have taken our last breath. What we do in the time between that moment and the present is what matters. Some people say that you should live every day as your last. While we understand the point, you must be careful that you don't just make impulsive decisions that could end up hurting your future.

You still have to plan for the future, but you want to be thankful for the decisions that led you to today. While preparing for your future, try not to overthink and plan everything out to the tee. You don't know what troubles or opportunities tomorrow will bring, so you just have to find a balance and do the best you can in the present.

Where You Spend Your Time Determines Your Success

If you spend a lot of time doing something, you will most likely become really good at it. If you use your time to play video games, you will probably be very good at playing them. If you use your time to study or learn a specific skill set, then you will be really good at that. You need to decide what you want to be good at and spend your time doing that thing. Video games and watching TV might be fun, and we know anything is possible, but there are very few people that find success in life by filling their time with these things. There are some things in life that don't reap any benefit, and these things should never take up the bulk of your time.

Spending your time learning, reading, and growing yourself are great activities for your spare time. You will develop skills and learn things that can be applied in life and increase your success levels. If you spend your time improving your math skills, you may not become a mathematician, but it is a valuable skill to have if you decide to open a business and need to track your money. The things you choose to spend your time on will determine how successful you become, so aim to do things that will grow you and make you a better person.

Who You Spend Your Time With Determines What Your Life Will Look Like

As kids, we are always told to choose our friends wisely. As we grow up, this instruction seems to take a back seat in our lives. We choose to be friends with whoever crosses our path, and we aren't really picky in this aspect. As adults, we need to get into the habit of being selective with our friends. Who we hang out with influences us more than anything else in life. We are more likely to make bad decisions if we are in the company of people who are making bad decisions.

When teenagers go to university, some of them go wild, and others put their heads down and study. These two groups of people don't really mingle with each other. The ones who study hard are surrounded by other people who study hard, and the ones who party all night are surrounded by people who do the same. When a student walks into university, they have to choose who they want to hang out with. Once they do that, they become like the group they choose to be around. It is very difficult to be studious when all your friends are out partying. In fact, it is almost impossible. Naturally, we want to do what our friends are doing, and eventually, we start thinking like them.

Before you make friends with a group of people, look at their lifestyle and ask yourself if that is something you want for yourself. If the answer is no, then you should distance yourself a bit and find people who live the way you want to live. Choose to be friends with people who challenge and inspire you—

people who work hard and want to work to reach their goals. If you partner up with these kinds of people, you will find that you will become like them. Successful people are always friends with other successful people.

You Need Time to Take Care of Yourself

We have been speaking a lot about using your time wisely. One of the most important things you can do is to take a little time to relax and focus on yourself. Many people forget about this on their journey to success. You need to be at your best physically and mentally if you want to be successful in any area of your life. This is why you shouldn't waste your time on things that don't give you a good result. Aim to spend your time wisely so that you have some time to spare to take care of yourself. Life is not worth living if you work all the time and leave no time for anything fun or relaxing.

Anything Worth Doing Takes Time

We live in an age where everything is moving at a breakneck pace. We want our daily commute, shopping, and everyday activities to be done quickly. This can be good in some areas, but it does not work all the time. You see, the most essential things in life take time to accomplish. You can't get your degree in a week; you have to spend four painstaking years in university and pour a lot of yourself into your courses before coming out on the other side with a degree. You can't expect to have the best marriage after putting in a day's worth of effort; you have to put in consistent effort for the long term.

If we live life thinking that things will always happen quickly, we won't want to put in any long-term effort. This will result in us missing the best things in life. We must all understand that just because something takes a long time to complete does not mean that it is a waste of time. As long as you make sure the things you put your time into are worth it in the end, spending that time will be completely worth it.

Effective Time Management is the Key to Success

Time is a crucial resource in our toolkit for success. If we use it wisely, we will be rewarded with success and a fulfilling life. If we squander our time, then we will end up in a situation that we do not want to be in. Once we learn how to manage our time effectively, we will be able to live our lives in the best way possible.

The fact is that we cannot control time. We can only learn how to manage it effectively. Throughout this book, there are many points interwoven into each habit on how to manage your time properly to yield the best results. Once you master these skills, you will be well on your way to living a more fulfilling and fruitful life.

3

DAILY DISCIPLINES

After embracing the first four habits, your mornings should be a jump start to your day. Once you've started your morning off well, you'll need to carry it on throughout the rest of the day. The middle portion of your day is where the majority of your responsibilities need to be taken care of. Aiming to be the most productive you can be will allow you to have days that are far less stressful and nights where you can just unwind and relax. Having this balance requires preparation.

Habits 5 through 10 will teach you how to make the most out of your days so that you can be more productive than you thought you ever could be. It's incredible how a few small habits can make such a massive difference in your day-to-day life. When you are more productive in the blocks you should be working, and it allows you to free up time for you to do other things. You can then choose what you want to do with that free time.

Everyone could do with a bit of extra free time to do something they are passionate about or even just taking some time to relax. At least, we haven't met anyone who would turn down the opportunity of that extra free time.

HABIT 5: ALWAYS CARRY A NOTEBOOK

How many times have you thought of a brilliant idea or a task that you have to get done but pushed it aside because you were busy with something else? We believe every single person does this at least once or twice a day. My next question is, did you remember that idea when you had the time to think about it? Probably not. Most of us believe that our minds are like steel traps that will save all of our thoughts until we have time to deal with them. The truth is that our minds are more like an open field, and once the thought starts to float away, you are going to have a hard time getting it back.

Carrying around a notebook with you is one of the best ways to document your thoughts. Most of our most extraordinary thoughts and ideas come to us when we least expect them. Successful people make sure they have a notebook with them at all times so that they never miss a brilliant idea. Some people say that their best ideas come to them when they first wake up or when they are about to go to bed. If they do not have a notebook within arm's reach, that idea will be lost forever because nobody has the energy to flesh out an idea when they are in bed. If you think that you don't have any good ideas or thoughts, try writing down anything that pops into your head throughout the day. You will be surprised at how many good ideas can come out of random thoughts. Just know that some of them will be duds, as we can't be brilliant all the time.

This is not the only benefit of carrying around a notebook with you. You will be able to retain information better when you write it down. There is always something to learn in the world around you. When you take notes of important things people say or new things that you learn, you will be able to remember them better. There is just something about taking the time to write something down that makes it stick in your head. Even if you never read your notes, you will still retain the information at a much higher level than if you just heard it and did nothing with it. Plus, it will save you a lot of time trying to remember something if you just have the information written down and on hand.

If you don't take notes in seminars, meetings, and classes, then you are missing out on getting the most out of those situations. When you take notes, you are forcing yourself to listen actively. I'm sure you have been in a meeting or class, and halfway through, you realize you did not hear a word the person was saying because you completely zoned out. We don't have a long attention span if we are not doing anything. We have to be physically doing something in order for us to be paying attention because it helps us focus our minds on the task. Taking down notes also allows you to capture what really matters. People speak faster than we are able to write, so we have to filter that information and only write down what is essential. This helps us build the skill of filtering out what is unimportant so that we only retain the things that matter. In life, this is so important because a lot of stuff that goes on around us is just white noise, and we must be able to hone in on what really matters.

Having a notebook handy also helps you get your thoughts out of your head and onto paper. I'm sure there have been a few times when you have been working on something, and you realize that there is something else that you need to get done. You tell yourself that you will do it later, but it is almost impossible to get that thought out of your mind. This leads to you not being effective in the task you are supposed to be doing. This distraction means that you are not as productive as you should be.

As soon as you write down that thought, you will find that you don't think about it all the time. This is because you know that you won't forget it and have done something to action that thought. You can then finish whatever you are busy with and then address what is in your notebook afterward. You will probably find that whatever you wrote down is not as urgent as you thought it was at that moment, and you have saved yourself from wasting your time. This is such a great tip that most people think will never work, but we are often working against our own minds. Once we figure out ways to calm our minds down and stop distracting ourselves with unimportant things, productivity increases exponentially.

Yeah, we know what a lot of you are thinking right now..." I'll just put it in my phone." While embracing technology is a beautiful thing, we've learned this habit from some of the most successful people, who frequently are pillars in technological fields (Richard Branson, for example). So just give it a shot, and find it for yourself. You'll be a lot less distracted jotting notes down in a planner or notebook than you will be typing into your phone or tablet.

HABIT 6: IDENTIFY THE "MIT" AND ALWAYS PRIORITIZE IT

"MIT" stands for the most important task. It might seem like a no-brainer to get the thing that is the most important done first, but most of us aren't inherently good at it. We are good at switching from one task to the next because each new task seems more important than the last. If we are constantly switching between tasks, we will never be able to manage our time and get stuff done effectively.

When we think of productivity, we automatically assume that it means getting as much stuff done as we can in a certain amount of time. This should not be the definition of productivity because getting a lot of stuff done does not mean that you are actually progressing. For example, if you have a big presentation to do for work or university, that is most likely your most important task. There may be other tasks that you need to get done, like organizing your closet, washing your car, answering emails, or getting to some general office filing. All of these tasks have their place, but when you stand up to give your presentation, the fact that you got all of those other things done and did not prepare for the presentation is going to bite you in the behind. While doing busy work, we can feel like we are productive, but we are really just keeping ourselves occupied with things that are not going to help us reach our ultimate goal.

James Clear, the author of the best-selling book *Atomic Habits*, says it brilliantly—productivity is getting important things done consistently. Even if you only get one thing done, if it's the most important thing, then you have been productive. The truth is that there usually are only a few really important things that you would need to get done in a day or even a week. The important things are going to reap the most benefit in your life, and that is why they have to be prioritized. All the other things can be squeezed into other pockets of time when you don't have any of these prioritized things being accomplished.

You shouldn't always aim to try and squeeze a whole bunch of tasks into a small space of time in an effort to be productive. If you do this consistently, you are on your way to significant burnout. Maintaining a steady pace of doing things that actually matter is what is going to bring you success. The best strategy for this is to start with those important things we just talked about first. It is so easy to get carried away with the day that you lose track of time and just don't end up getting to the tasks that really matter. When you set aside time to do those things first, you know they are done and out of the way. As the day wears on and other lower priority tasks start popping up, you can do them with the assurance that those really important things are already knocked out.

Let's just be honest here—the things that are the most important are often the things that are either the most difficult or the most boring to do. This is why we procrastinate about them. If there is a way to get out of doing something hard, naturally, we will take it. In the morning, we have the most amount of willpower, which means that we are more likely to do the hard things earlier in the day. As it gets closer to the afternoon, it becomes harder to convince ourselves to do unpleasant things. The other benefit of doing the hard stuff earlier in the day is that once we start, there is a much higher likelihood of us finishing them. For most of us, we have an affinity to finish what we have started. Once we get the momentum going, we can carry that through until the task is completed.

HABIT 7: BE YOUR OWN PARENT—LIMIT YOUR SCREEN TIME

It is no lie that technology has come with a ton of benefits. We can get in contact with loved ones at the press of a button, communication has never been more accessible, entertainment is right at our fingertips, and we have access to all the information in the world right in the palm of our hand. This has opened up so many doors and made us more advanced as a civilization than ever before, but there are things we should be cautious with when it comes to our use of certain kinds of technology. Like everything else in life, there are some disadvantages.

The best-known way to be productive is to enter something called a flow state. This is where you can sit for a particular block of time and just get work done. Your mind is entirely focused on the task, and you can just run with it. If you are trying to be productive, you should be trying to limit distractions so that you enter the flow state. It takes a while to get into the flow of things, and once you are distracted, you have to get your mind back into that state again. It can take about 20 to 30 minutes to focus your mind again after it has been distracted.

Our phones are the biggest distractions in our life. As soon as you hear that notification, you want to check your phone. It is almost like an immediate reaction. Even just having your phone around you can be a distraction because when you see it, you want to pick it up just in case you have missed something. Think about how many notifications you get in a day. 20? 50? We know for some, it can be easily over a hundred notifications across different apps—that means there are a hundred various distractions provided by this little box you carry around with you everywhere you go.

When you are trying to get into a productive mindset and get a notification, you are immediately taken out of your flow. Even if you resist the urge to check your phone and just leave it, you have still removed your attention from the thing you were working on. Now you have to try and get back there, which, like we already mentioned, is going to take you at least 20 minutes. It's 20 minutes of being a lot less productive because you are preparing yourself to do your task. Can you see how this is a problem for your productivity? It may only take you 30 seconds to check the notification, but you are consistently losing out on 20 to 30 minutes of peak productivity. That is a lot of time that you are wasting when you add it up.

The only way you can stop yourself from losing this time is to remove the distraction. You can put your phone on airplane mode when you're working so that you don't receive any notifications. If you don't hear anything, you won't know when a notification comes in, and then you won't be tempted to check. Another great option is to remove your phone from your workspace altogether. Either put it in a drawer, leave it in your bag, or place it in another room. Sometimes having it on silent is not enough because if it is in your line of vision, you might be tempted to pick it up. Many of us don't realize that phones are really addictive and can be a significant contributor to a lack of productivity.

DAILY HABIT EVOLUTION

Besides just making sure that you are not distracted by your phone, you should also be conscious about how much time you spend on it as a whole. There are a whole bunch of negatives that come with being too attached to your phone. The truth is that you don't actually need it as much as you think you do. Once you separate yourself from it, you will see that you can function quite well without knowing what everyone else is doing all the time. Social media is something that most people have, and it has captured people's time and attention more than anything else in the world. I'm sure you have been down the Facebook, Instagram, YouTube, and TikTok rabbit hole. You started off only wanting to check something for five minutes, and suddenly you look up, and you have been scrolling or watching for two hours. This can be a massive waste of time, especially when you have something important to get done.

Social media also leads us to compare our lives to other people's lives. We can get so caught up in what we don't have that we demotivate ourselves. People tend to only post the good things on social media and not their everyday lives. We don't know about you, but we don't remember ever seeing an Instagram post about someone losing their job, being in debt, or having a fight with their significant other. However, the posts about overseas vacations, new cars, new houses, shopping sprees, and their outstanding relationships with significant others are plentiful on everyone's timeline. It's not that we should want the negative things to be posted on social media, but we should be looking at social media through the lens of "this is not the full picture." In any case, it is better to limit the time you are scrolling and looking at other people's lives so that you can focus on bettering your own life.

Most people don't know that they spend so much time on their phones. Most phones track your screen time, so you should definitely take a look at this and see how many hours you spend on your phone a day. You will probably be shocked when you see it. Most people guess that they have a screen time of about one hour, but it's something like three to five hours when they check. If you are on the lower end and spend three hours a day on your phone, it may not seem like that much, but let's put it into perspective. Three hours a day works out to 1,095 hours in a year. That is the equivalent of you staying up and spending time on your phone and not sleeping for a month and a half, every single year. That's excessive! Imagine how much you can get done in that time if you put the phone down.

You can check what apps are taking up most of your time so that you know what your biggest problem is. For most of us, it will be either social media or games. If that is the case, there are a few things you can do to help cut the bad habit and replace it with this new habit of limiting your screen time. The most drastic and often the most needed is to simply delete the apps that are taking away your time. If you don't have any self-control when it comes to this, then this is the best option. If you want to scroll on Instagram, you can plug the URL into your browser and do it that way. Since the interface is not as attractive, and it takes a bit of effort to get there, you won't be tempted to go on as much as you usually would be. You could also log out of the app, so if you mindlessly just click on the icon, you will be greeted with the log-in page instead of your timeline. Creating a bit of friction between you and your social media feed is all you need. It causes you to stop and think if going on social media is something you really want to do. When it comes to games, you will just have to delete them. You can redownload the app or game on the weekend or when you have free time to play, or simply limit games to a different device such as a tablet, computer, or gaming console. These are the best ways to make your phone less attractive to you and stop you from spending so much time on it.

HABIT 8: ONLY TOUCH IT ONCE

As you go through your workday, there are new things that pop up that need your attention. It really doesn't matter what your job is or even if you work for yourself. You will have multiple tasks popping up that you didn't expect. Now, once you get a new task to do, you have the choice of whether you want to do it now or leave it until later on. The problem with leaving it for later is that you will keep thinking about the new task until you do something about it.

Continuously leaving things for later is a form of procrastination. It impacts how productive you will be throughout the day. Most of the time, these ad hoc tasks will just take a few minutes out of our day. If we keep putting off a task, we will be wasting a lot more time thinking about it than if we actually just did it. In these cases, it is better to get it done so that it is off your plate. These ad hoc tasks that pop up are also why doing the most important things early in the morning is vital to your productivity for the rest of the day.

The only-touch-once rule is something that you can implement to stop procrastination and get these tasks done. We often don't want to do things that seem boring or mundane, so these are the types of tasks that we put off. When you implement the only-touch-once rule, when a task is in front of you, you have to take action to resolve the task at that moment. Even if you don't finish it, you have to make an actionable decision about that task.

Let's use an example to help better explain this. Say you are busy with your everyday work, and you get an email from your manager saying that you need to fetch a document, scan it, and email it to the relevant person. You will see the email, but you will not want to do that task or even answer the email if you are busy with something else. You will convince yourself that you have to finish what you are doing before you move on to something else. The problem is that you have already seen the email (which is the same as "touching" the task). So now, this new task will be playing on your mind until you do something about it. The best thing to do is just fetch the documents and email them, as long as the current task you are working on isn't a higher priority. This will only take a few minutes, and you can get back to what you were doing before. If what you are doing is really important and you cannot stop, simply email your manager and tell them that you will fetch the documents in a set amount of time because you are currently busy with something else, and then set a small reminder to not forget that task after you finish your current one.

The only-touch-once rule is not entirely about finishing things as they come in. It is about taking an actionable step towards completing the new task so that it isn't playing on your mind. Once you have told your manager that you will tend to their request in an hour, you can put it out of your mind until the hour is up. You have effectively decluttered your mental space so that you can entirely focus on what you are doing. This will save you so much time because you will probably be clicking in and out of that email many times if you don't do something about it. Once a task comes across your desk, decide what you are going to do with it. Even if you decide that you will do the task in two hours, having a plan means that you don't have to keep thinking about it, and your mind is free to concentrate on what you are supposed to be doing.

HABIT 9: IF IT TAKES LESS THAN TWO MINUTES, DO IT NOW

This habit can go hand in hand with habit 8. Most of the things we procrastinate about aren't actually hard. We just convince ourselves that we can't do it for whatever reason. We put things off and then regret it later. Now the two-minute rule has two very different parts and can be applied in different ways, but both are extremely helpful if you want to increase your productivity.

In the first application, if there is a task that you have to do and it can be done in under two minutes, just do it. The reality is that we think things will take much longer than they actually will. How many times have you not taken out the garbage because you convinced yourself that it could wait or procrastinated about sending an email because you had other things to do? These are such small things that can be done in no time at all, but we can put them off until they become a problem. You always have two minutes to spare, regardless of how busy you are.

The second application works with building habits and doing hard things. Forming new habits and completing challenging tasks are not things that are pleasant, and, therefore, we push them back as far as we can. The other problem that we have with this is that when we have something hard to do, we convince ourselves that we need a long period of time to do it. Let's say you want to start exercising every day. In most people's minds, you have to carve out 45 minutes to an hour to get in a workout. So, if you only have 15 to 30 minutes to spare, you can convince yourself that it is not worth doing, and you will just do it at another time. The reality is that a small amount of exercise is better than none at all, and when you are building a habit, what matters most is that you actually do something rather than doing it perfectly.

This type of mentality is needed when you implement the two-minute rule for doing hard things. We can all do something challenging and unpleasant for two minutes. It is easier to convince ourselves to do this unpleasant thing for a short amount of time than when we think of it as a mammoth task. If you want to start making a habit of reading, instead of thinking you have to read a chapter a day, tell yourself that you will just read the first few lines of a particular page. If you want to start learning a new language, instead of thinking you need to carve out one hour for an in-depth lesson, tell yourself that you are just going to learn one word. If you want to start going for a run every day, instead of committing yourself to a 30-minute run, just put your running shoes on and go stand outside.

Now you might be thinking that just putting on the running shoes and standing outside is not going to help you lose weight. To be fair, you would be correct, but once you make that small step, the chances are really high that you will actually go for that run. You see, the hardest part is just starting. Once you overcome that mental barrier that is blocking you from getting started, you will be able to continue with that hard thing. One line of reading will turn into a 30-minute session. Learning one word in another language will turn into learning entire sentences. Just putting your running shoes on will result in you taking that 30-minute jog.

It is almost like tricking yourself into doing something. Once you get started, it is easy to ride the momentum and just keep going. So even if the thing will take more than two minutes to complete, tell yourself that you will only do that task for two minutes, and then you can stop. You will find, more often than not, you will end up seeing that thing to completion. And even if you don't, you will have gotten a little closer to your goal, which is still a win. Two minutes is better than nothing!

HABIT 10: GOAL-DRIVEN ACTIONS

On a typical day, you probably have lots of different things being thrown at you. While you are at work, your friend calls you because they need some advice on something. You are going out for a much-needed date night with your significant other, and your boss calls you because there is some sort of problem that needs solving. In life, things keep moving, and the various parts of your life overlap. Even the same area can overlap on itself. For example, you are busy typing out a spreadsheet that needs to be submitted by the end of the day, and your colleague comes in and needs your help with an urgent matter.

When these things happen, they can very quickly derail us. Not only this, but we end up taking on so much that we aren't productive in anything. When you are at a crossroads with so many things vying for your attention, you need to decide what your goal is and what will help you get there. You only have so many hours in the day, and you need to be able to use them effectively to get the best results. If you try and split yourself all over the place, you will never be able to put your whole effort into the things that really matter.

In the above examples, you will need to ask yourself what your goals are and which task truly needs to be accomplished. From there, you can decide to say no to one thing so that you can accomplish something that will get you closer to your ultimate goal. In the first example, when you are at work and your friend calls, at that moment, you need to ask yourself, what is the goal? Chances are, your goal will be to finish the work that you have in front of you. If you take the time to speak to your friend, it will put you behind in your work, so that is not going to help you reach the goal. Based on this, you will have to tell your friend that you will call them later because you have to finish your work. The second example shows you that this is not only applicable to work situations. You can have goals in other areas, and this might require you to say no to work. If you have committed to having a date night because things have been pretty hectic and you just want to reconnect, that is the goal. If you answer your phone, it might derail you from meeting that goal. The best thing to do in this situation is to not answer the phone. Even if you don't know what will be asked of you, you do know that it might be something that will cause you to miss the date night. If the boss really needs something urgently, they will most likely send you a message, and you will be able to see what it is without being pressured to say yes to it when you are on the phone. There are always alternate ways to deal with situations that can save face in both areas.

Now in the scenario where both tasks are in the same arena, in this case, both work-related, you have to figure out what is going to best serve both your goals and those of the company. You need to ask yourself if the spreadsheet is more important or if your colleague's issue matters more. In most cases, when someone comes in and asks for your help, it is something that can wait, or they can go and ask someone else. Your ultimate goal will be to complete your work. These are the tasks that your employer has trusted you with, and if they do not get done, you will get flack for it. Unless the problem that your colleague needs help with will impact the company as a whole or the person negatively, you don't have to help them right now. You will have to tell your colleague that you cannot help at that present time, but you will do your best to revisit their issue once you get to a stopping point. This isn't always the easiest to do, but with a clearer mind from implementing some of these other habits, you should be able to decipher which situation needs your attention most.

Those were all pretty big situations where you had to possibly step on someone's toes in order to stay on track with your goals. It is important to know what to do in those situations. You aren't saying no as a whole, but you are putting off the peripheral tasks until you have the time and the space to complete them. You will call your friend back, find out what your boss needs, and help your colleague, but not right at that moment. The bigger goal is more important than the distractions that come about.

In your average day, you probably won't come across many situations where you need to stand your ground and be firm with the people around you to meet your goals. Most of the time, you are your worst enemy, so you'll have to use the firmness you use with other people on yourself. If you find yourself being overwhelmed by the number of tasks you have, you will need to take a second to pause. You can write down everything you think you need to get done, then pick the things that you know will help you reach your ultimate goal for the day. For example, if you have a presentation coming up tomorrow, reading through emails, doing admin tasks, and working on the project that is due next week should not be on your to-do list right now. You can do those things after the presentation is done and you have the time to realign your goals. Doing things in this order is what will bring you the most success. So before you do anything, ask yourself the question, "Is this going to get me closer to my goal?"

If you are the type of person who goes into your day without knowing what your goals are, this habit is going to be really hard to implement. The first thing you should do every morning is sit down and decide what your goal or goals will be for the day. This way, when things start popping up, or you feel like you need to complete a task, you have something to measure it against. If you don't know what your goal is for the day, there is no way of telling if you are accomplishing something or just going with the flow of the day. Having clearly defined goals is how you win in life.

HABIT 11: DON'T OVERCOMPLICATE THINGS

We all have a tendency to overcomplicate things. When you first start out a project and begin to plan out the process, you probably take liberties with your time and resources. This is where you start color-coding, trying to fit everything in place, outlining, and doing everything else that isn't actually part of completing the project. Contrast this to when you have a deadline that is looming. There is no structuring or overplanning. You just do it, and you do it as fast as you can. Most people actually say they work better under pressure. It's not the pressure that helps them work better. It's the fact that having limited time means that you have to simplify the process in order to get the job done.

Overcomplicating things is a waste of time. Most things in life don't need that much planning because when you get there, the plan will change. We all think that we can foresee what will happen in the future and plan for it, but this is hardly the case. Throughout this book, you have been learning about the habits that will lead you to success. You might feel tempted to plan out how you will implement them and see how they are going to fit into your life. Can we encourage you just to do it? Don't overthink or overcomplicate things. Taking action is the most important thing. You can always readjust throughout the process. When you start something, it doesn't have to be all figured out.

If you have a task in front of you and you have a tendency to overcomplicate things, then we would suggest first visualizing what you have to do. This is where that notebook will come in handy. When you write down the problem and see it in front of you, it is easier to sort through your thoughts. You can rule out the things that are not important in this scenario and focus on the things that are. Often when we have a big task or project in front of us, we tend to think about a million different things that could be related to what we have to do. This is what makes us feel overwhelmed. If you are feeling this way, you need to write down everything you are thinking. Look it over and see what you can take action on right now. Chances are most of the things you are thinking about can't be done right now, or you may not even be capable of doing them yourself. Highlight the things that you can do and focus on those. The other things on the list are either things you can't control or are not important at this moment.

Simplifying your strategy or approach to something can be difficult if you are in the trenches. In order to know how to simplify something, you need to get the complete picture of it. Stepping back and looking at the problem or project as a whole will help you to understand what needs to be done to get it resolved. It will help you hone in on the parts that will get you the results you want instead of focusing on things that don't really matter.

Simplifying this can be a struggle. It is not something that we inherently know how to do, but it is a skill that will put us above the rest. It will help us do more meaningful work that will actually get us somewhere instead of just doing everything. The major problem with most people in the workforce is that they just do whatever comes across their desk without thinking about it. The work you do has to get you closer to your goal, and if it doesn't, then it might not be worth your time. Whether you are employed by someone or your work for yourself, your job has a function. If you fully understand what that function is, you can structure out your tasks and simplify your work life in order to meet that function.

So ultimately, habits 10 and 11 coincide and help each other. To increase your productivity, even more, it will take simplifying the process, so you don't overwhelm your mind, but you also have to put some thought into which actions help you reach your goals.

Help! I Can't Decide

When you are trying to simplify things, you need to be able to make decisions. You need to decide what is important and what is not. Often we can think everything is important and then waste our time doing things that really don't matter in the grand scheme. Remember, you only have a certain number of hours in the day. It is up to you to decide how to use those hours. Your decisions will either make you successful and productive or just another mindless cog in the machine of society.

Most people sit and agonize over the small things and then let the big things just happen. For example, we can spend a good hour deciding what to make for dinner or what to watch on Netflix, but when it comes to having children or moving to a new city, it can just happen on a whim. Life would be much simpler and better if we took the time to think about the big things and not spend so much time trying to make decisions about things that are of little to no consequences in the long run.

The problem with big decisions is that we often make them under conditions that are not suitable. We feel pressured in the moment, and then we just make the decision without having a chance to fully think things through. We know a fair share of people who have moved cities, or even countries, and then a few months later completely regretted it. When they made this decision, they were swept up in the excitement of going somewhere new, they got caught up with the advertising, or they listened to someone else and based their decision on that.

The other problem that we have with decision-making is that we are often moved by emotion. We adopt a dog because we feel so bad that it is living in a shelter. Then when we bring it home, we realize that we don't have the facilities for it or are financially stretched because we didn't work dog expenses into the budget. Some people take jobs at non-profits or charity organizations because they want to make a difference and then later realize that the salary is not enough to sustain them. It is not that any of these decisions are inherently wrong. However, they can be if you are not aware of what they entail, and you can end up in a situation that you do not want to be in.

Alright, so now we know why making decisions is so important, but how do we make the right ones? In life, there are two extremes to decision-making. One is procrastination, overthinking, and ultimately avoiding making the decision. The other is just diving in and making the decision on a whim. The key to decision-making is striking a balance between the two. If you need to make a decision, you will need the right strategy.

Firstly, when you need to make a big decision, you need the time to do so. Often we can feel so pressured to decide that we just do it on the spot. This is never a good idea. What you should do is remove yourself from the situation and give yourself time to think. If someone is pressuring you to decide at that moment, that should be a red flag to you. You have to make sure you are weighing your options and that you are not making a decision based on emotions. The amount of time could range anywhere from just a few moments all the way up to days, weeks, or months. It's not so much about a defined amount of time, but rather that you gave yourself uninfluenced time to logically make the decision instead of emotionally making it.

Next, you need to understand what you are saying yes to and what you are saying no to. For example, if you take a new job, you are saying yes to making more money and advancing your career, but you may be saying no to family time or to starting a side hustle. Every decision has these kinds of pros and cons. If you want to make the right decision, you will need to understand it from every angle to get the complete picture of what life will look like after the decision has been made.

Lastly, you need to give yourself a deadline. Overthinking and procrastinating about decisions makes the process harder. If you don't have a set date that you need to provide your answer by, you will never make the decision. Give yourself enough time to think about it, do some research, and talk to the relevant people, but don't leave it open-ended. Having a set date is like making a commitment to yourself, and you will want to honor that.

When you are making a decision, it helps to talk to others about it. Now, don't go talking to any person who will listen. You should be talking to people who you trust and who might have some experience in the field you are trying to make a decision in. Too many voices can drown out your own voice, so be careful with this. Don't speak to too many people. Pick a few close friends or mentors who you know and trust, gain their input, and then it's up to you.

Sometimes, though, you really do just have to trust your gut. If you are forcing yourself into something, there is a high chance that you are making the wrong decision. Some things are just against our values or what we want out of life, but we are scared to say no because the opportunity sounds good. If you have to force yourself to go ahead with something, then there is probably a reason for it. Flesh out your feelings and get to the root of them. From there, you will be able to make a better decision. At the end of the day, any decision is better than none at all. Just leaving something hanging in the air is going to haunt you until you do something about it. This is going to be a distraction, and you won't be able to focus on your day-to-day tasks. Follow the advice given to you here, and you should be well on your way to being a pro-decision-maker.

4

CONSTANT CONTROL VS. CONSTANT CHANGE

In this chapter, we will be discussing the principle of time blocking or time boxing. It is something that many successful people use to organize their day and help them be more productive. It is something that will help you implement all the other habits that have been mentioned. Utilizing these ideas will create a structure that will set you up for success in your work and personal life.

WHAT IS TIME BLOCKING?

We are all familiar with goal setting. Most of us find it relatively easy to set a goal for the day. However, it's the getting there that gives us a bit of a problem. It often seems like we don't have enough time to get things done, or the day just runs away from us. It can be incredibly frustrating to feel like you are doing work, but it doesn't seem like you are getting anything done when you look up. Most people attribute this feeling to not having enough hours in the day or having too much work on their plate, but it actually might be a time management issue.

Throughout this book, we've spoken about the importance of time management. When you manage your time effectively, you are able to accomplish all your work tasks and have some free time just to relax and do the things you enjoy. Time management is the key to a well-balanced life. Unfortunately, most people aren't very good at it. Time blocking is one of the best answers to the riddle of time management.

Time blocking asks you to divide up your day into specific blocks of time. Each block is dedicated to a particular task and nothing else. It is like creating a to-do list, but each task has a place in your day. Instead of just trying to squeeze tasks in, you have purposely carved out time for each task. Using this method allows you to see what is most important and schedule your days according to your energy levels.

The key to effective time blocking is to put each task in the right place and to give yourself the right amount of time to complete it. Your first block of time should be for your most important task and the one that will take you the most amount of time. This will allow you to concentrate for longer, and there are fewer distractions earlier in the day than in the afternoons. Things that require less brain power can be left for the afternoons. We have all experienced an afternoon slump where we feel drained and sluggish. This is not the ideal time to do deep work. Instead, put busy work into this slot.

Here is an example of a time blocked workday:

8 a.m.	Work on presentation
9 a.m.	
10 a.m.	
11 a.m.	Answer emails/phone calls/admin
12 p.m.	
1 p.m.	Lunch and social media
2 p.m.	Meetings
3 p.m.	
4 p.m.	Training session
5 p.m.	Overflow

You can see that everything has its place. You know what you have to do and how much time you have for each task. The trick is to make sure that you allocate the right amount of time for each task. You'd rather have given too much time than too little time. We often think that we can do things faster than we actually can. It might take a few days before you can accurately gauge how long each task will take, so be patient when you first start time blocking.

You will notice at the bottom of the graphic there is an hour that is allocated to overflow. This is the time that you can finish up anything that you weren't able to during the day. So if you still have a few more emails to respond to or you need to add the final touches to the presentation, you have time to do that. The overflow time is needed every day because sometimes things will take longer than expected. Instead of pushing your whole day back, have a time specifically to go back to the tasks you didn't finish.

The above schedule also has time for a break and social media. No human has the ability to sit and do work for all hours of the workday. We need a break from time to time, and it is important to schedule it in. It is not indicated above, but you will need to take at least a five- to ten-minute break before jumping into the next thing when you switch between tasks. That is why it might seem that there is a lot of time allocated to each task, but you need to take into account the task-switching time and a short break. You will find that you work much better if you give your brain a chance to rest every now and then.

You will also see in the above example that there are a few tasks that are grouped together. Grouping similar tasks together can help when planning out your day. Answering emails, phone calls, and admin are all tasks that are not set in stone. On some days, you will have lots of emails, and on others, only a few. If you don't have lots of emails, you can dedicate more time to doing your general admin tasks. This creates a bit of flexibility even though you are still sticking to a strict time-blocked schedule. The overflow time also gives you time to deal with any unexpected tasks that may pop up. As much as we would like days to go according to our schedule, life doesn't work like that. We need to account for some sort of unexpected scenarios. If you don't end up using the overflow time, then you have some extra time to do what you want, so there really isn't a downside to this.

You can take time blocking further by blocking out your entire day. This will show when you have time to relax, read, work on a side hustle, or spend time with your friends and family. If you are someone who struggles to prioritize their personal life, this will help you. You have set out time to do these things, so you don't have to feel guilty for taking some time for yourself at the end of the day.

There is another form of time blocking that can work for people whose days do not have many tasks going on. It is called day theming. All you have to do is set out each day of the week for a specific task. So if you are a videographer, Monday will be for planning the shoot, Tuesday for filming, Wednesday for editing, Thursday for meetings, and Friday for admin. This might not work for everyone, but if you are someone who has a lot of different things that compete for your attention, you can use this to your advantage. You can take the whole day and just focus on one task at a time and get it off your plate.

THE BENEFITS OF TIME BLOCKING

If you are unable to control your schedule, it will control you. A day without a plan is one that runs away from you. It takes you for a ride instead of you having a set purpose for the day. As many people say, failing to plan is planning to fail. The most successful people in the world don't have the luxury of wasting a day. They have to be productive because they have lots of other people counting on them. This is why people like Elon Musk, Bill Gates, and productivity expert Cal Newport time block their day. If these big-named business people use time blocking, there must be some serious benefit to it.

Having a Plan Motivates You

Going into your day blindly is a recipe for unproductivity. You don't know what the important tasks are, so it becomes impossible to prioritize and work well. Time blocking is like creating a blueprint for your day. You know what you are supposed to be doing, and you know when you should be doing it.

When you have something written down and scheduled, it creates a sense of importance around it. You are more likely to make sure that it gets done because you have committed yourself to it. This is why people schedule meetings and appointments. You will often find people running out of the office to make their meetings because it is something important. You create the same time of mentality around all your tasks.

You Can Schedule According to Your Energy Levels

If you pay attention to yourself, you will see that your energy levels shift during the day. The most common is high energy in the morning, an afternoon energy slump after lunch, and then energy picks back up towards the end of the day. Since every person is different, your energy levels might look different. For the type of person described above, it would be wise to do the most essential tasks in the morning and then leave the busy work tasks for the afternoon. Towards the end of the day, they can do things a little more important, like meetings and planning.

Once you understand how your energy levels fluctuate throughout the day, you will be able to plan effectively. Instead of working against your body, you will be working with it. This is a much more effective plan, and it is much healthier than filling yourself up with caffeine to try and make it through a period of low energy.

Time Blocking Removes the Decisions and Distractions

When you time block, you become laser-focused on the task in front of you. This is because you have already allocated time for the other things in your life. There aren't a million things fighting for your attention because they all have their place. Here's an example. If a doctor had an open-door policy, people would be fighting to get to see the doctor first. Everyone thinks that their issue is the most important, so they all want the doctor to pay attention to them first. There might be screaming, pushing, shoving, and maybe the occasional punch, just to get the first block of time with the doctor. The doctor has to decide which one is the most critical patient to see first, so you can imagine that it won't go well for the doctor. Now, if the doctor has appointments, the whole situation is a lot more civilized. People will calmly wait their turn because they know that they will get seen, and they know precisely when they are going to have time with the doctor. The people are your tasks, and you are the doctor. Not scheduling causes havoc in your day-to-day life.

In life, when there are lots of tasks that need to be completed, they are all at odds with one another in your mind. You don't know which one to focus on, so you get distracted. You have to constantly decide what the most important thing to get done is at the moment, and often, you will get it wrong. It is tough to make those decisions when everything seems important. Time blocking means that all the decisions have been made for you. All you have to do is sit down and do the work at the allotted time. You won't have to argue with yourself about what deserves your attention next because you would already know.

Time Blocking Allows You to Do Deep Work

The term deep work was coined by productivity expert Cal Newport. He wrote a whole book on the subject, and it has helped many people increase their productivity. The premise of deep work is to get into a space where there are no distractions, and you push your cognitive abilities to their limit. This is where new ideas are born, work is produced at great speed, and the quality of your work will be the best.

Have you ever been so engrossed in a task that you have basically zoned out from the rest of the world? You can sit and do that one thing for hours, and you aren't bored or tired. The chances are that you were in a state of deep work. Your mind was focused on one thing, and you were able to be highly productive in a short space of time. The general consensus is that you can complete a whole day's worth of work in a few hours if you have entered a space of deep work.

When you time block, you are creating a space for deep work to take place. You are only focusing on one task and nothing else. You have created the environment for your brain to be focused entirely on that one thing, and that is the space of productivity. Multitasking, when it comes to truly important tasks, isn't what people make it out to be. No one can actually effectively multitask and accomplish things to the same level of quality because our brains are not designed in that way. If you want to be productive, you have to focus on doing one thing at a time and doing it really well.

You Will Get More Done in a Short Amount of Time

Parkinson's law states that work expands so as to fill the time available for its completion (The Wealth Advisor, 2019). This means that if you give yourself two weeks to do a task, that is how long it will take you to get it done. If you give yourself two hours to do a task, you will finish it in that time. Procrastination exists when we have too much time on our hands. It is the reason most people only study the week of their exams even though they have an entire semester to study.

Once you have given yourself a set time to do something, you are more likely to finish it in that time. Even if you don't complete the whole task, you will be far closer than if you just left it open-ended. Structure saves you so much time, and then you have more time to do things that you want to do and that matter to you.

Time Blocks Help You Say No

If you are a nice guy, you know how hard it is to say no. If you work in an office environment, you will most likely have people coming in and asking you to do tasks. These tasks may not form part of your job, and people are just asking you to do them because they don't want to. This means that your work gets put on the back burner.

When you time block, you will immediately know whether you have time to help someone else out or not. You will also know at what point in the day you are available to help. It allows you to say no because you are already engaged with another task. You can communicate to the other person that you can help out in your free time or the time allocated to overflow but just not right now. This allows you to be productive in your own space.

5

EMBRACE THE END (OF YOUR DAY)

How you finish your day is just as important as how you started it. It can actually be argued that it is even more important than how you start your day. The reason is that if you end your day badly, the following day will be a reflection of that. If you do not get time to relax in the evening and instead stay up late working, you will be tired, demotivated, and unable to concentrate the next morning. This is not the recipe for a successful day.

There is a lot more to your evenings than just getting a good night's rest. The evening is the time for you to prepare for the next day. It sets you up for future success. If you get it right, you will be able to unwind and relax but also set your next day up in the best way possible.

HABIT 12: CALM YOUR MIND AS THERE IS ALWAYS MORE TO DO

At the end of the day, when all your work is done, you might feel like you have not done enough, or maybe you just want to do one more thing before you rest. The thing is that there will always be more to do. Once the day ends, it doesn't mean that everything you need to do is actually done. However, getting caught up in that mindset prevents us from really taking time to relax. Trying to get it all done or be perfect can quickly lead to burnout. You must understand that there is a time for work, and there is a time for rest. These areas affect each other. If you rest well, you will be able to work well, and if you perform well, you can have a peaceful rest.

There is endless opportunity to get better and improve yourself. Just because you aren't working 24/7 doesn't mean that you will miss out on a chance to be your best self. You should have a balanced outlook on life. If you feel anxious about where you are in life, remember that there is always more to come. Albert Einstein's famous quote says, "The more I learn, the more I realize how much I don't know." The better we get, the more we realize that we have a long way to go. So if you are not content with where you are, just know that you are further than you were yesterday. This is what made you realize that there is so much further to go, and you should be proud of where you are. There will always be another step, but you should be able to really enjoy where you are as well.

You might be eager to step into the next phase of your life or want to take on new challenges. This is a great attitude to have but remember to make the most of the opportunities you have now. Calm your mind down so that you can be present in the current space you are in. There are plenty of things that you can do to make sure that you are improving where you are.

The evenings are a time for yourself, and there are things that you can do that will help in the future but will still keep you grounded in the now. It is essential to have this balance as it will give you clarity and motivation for the future.

Always Look for Opportunities to Learn

The world is filled with opportunities to learn something new. Learning is one of our greatest blessings. It forces us to think differently and expand our world view. It is so important to be a student of life. Every day should be a learning and growing experience. This is what challenges you and inspires you for the future.

Learning also has a calming effect on us. When we are listening to someone teach us something or working on a new skill, it takes us out of our every day and makes us focus on something else. The other benefit of learning is that you can step into a new day with more knowledge than you had the day before. You will be able to reason differently and maybe find a new solution to a problem.

When people learn, they often focus on learning things in the field they are in. Accountants take courses to become better accountants. Public speakers watch other speakers to understand how they do things. This is all great, but there are benefits to learning things that are not in your field. You may not know how it is going to come in handy, but it definitely can. The best ideas come from people who link two completely foreign ideas. Nothing you learn will ever go to waste.

Positive Discontentment

If you want to be better than you were the day before, you have to have a sense of positive discontentment. You should always be proud of what you accomplished, but it shouldn't just stop there. You should not just accept that where you are now is the end goal. There is more to come, and you can push yourself to get there.

Evenings are the perfect time to do some self-evaluation. You should not be your own critic, but just take some time to go over the day. Pick out a few areas that you thought you really excelled in and be proud of that. Then pick a few areas that you think you can improve in. Nobody is perfect, so no matter how old you get, there will always be room for improvement. Knowing the areas, you can improve in makes you conscious of them. If you don't know what you can be doing better, you will never get better in the long run.

When you are evaluating your day, see what worked and what didn't work. Do more of the things that did work, and understand why the other things didn't work. From here, you can make a plan to change. You can switch around your schedule or try out a new routine. Eventually, you will be able to make your day work for you in the best way possible. This is only possible if you have a sense of positive discontentment.

Be Better Than You Were Yesterday

In life, we can always improve. It is one of the only things that we can be sure of. We will mess up, and we will fail, but that is just life. If you had a particularly bad day today, then your goal should be to do better tomorrow. You don't have to change your whole lifestyle if something didn't work. Just plan to be a little bit better than the day before. Small, incremental steps towards bettering yourself are sustainable and will result in long-term changes. You may not feel as though you are making a huge difference, but when you look back from where you came, you will see that the gap is much more significant than what you thought. That is something to be proud of.

Remember that you shouldn't be competing with anyone else. You aren't trying to be better than Susan from down the road. You are just trying to better yourself. As soon as you start comparing yourself to every other person, you set yourself up for failure. Your life is not the same as theirs, and you don't know what they had to do or go through to get where they are. It's not fair on yourself to play the comparison game. Besides, you will never improve yourself if you are constantly looking at what other people are doing.

HABIT 13: PLAN MEALS AHEAD

Meal planning is one of the most significant habits you can get into. Not only will it save you time and money, but it will also help you get healthier. We don't think there is any person that does not want all three of those things in their life. These days, we are swamped, and there isn't a lot of time for us to make good meals. This results in us eating a lot of quick and unhealthy meals. Fast food is the go-to for many people, but it can really burn a hole in your pocket and negatively impact your health in the long term.

Meal planning is just deciding what you are going to be eating before the meal time arrives. You can take time once or twice a week to think about what you are going to be eating for the next few days. Once you know what you want to eat, you can buy those specific groceries, then meal prep. This means cooking what you can in advance to save you time when it is time for your meal.

You can meal plan and prep for every single meal of the day without too much difficulty. It dramatically lessens the time you will be standing in the kitchen, and you will also spend less time trying to think about what to eat. I'm sure you have spent a good couple of minutes staring at the contents of your fridge, trying to think about what to eat that day, only to decide to make a sandwich or order in. Planning is the solution to that problem.

The evenings are a great time to meal plan and prep because you have some extra time on your hands. It is also a great way to unwind. Cooking can be a great way to de-stress. You could also do this on the weekend or whenever you have the time to do so. There is really no hard and fast rule as to when you should meal plan, and how simple or complex you make the recipes is up to you.

Creating Your Meal Plan and Prep

Meal planning is easy once you get the hang of it. Most of us don't cook brand new and exciting meals every single day, so don't put too much pressure on yourself when you first start meal planning. Think about what you like to eat and make that. You should also account for leftovers and things that you will be eating more than once during the week. If you write down your plan and you see that rice is in two or more of your meals, make a big batch of rice and keep it in the fridge. This way, you are not wasting your time cooking rice three separate times in the week.

Start off by planning your breakfast for the week. Many people skip breakfast because they are in a rush in the morning, but we need the energy breakfast gives us to fuel our day. Rather than missing it, prepare it in the evening so that you can just grab and go. Breakfast burritos (egg, lettuce, cheese, and bacon in a wrap) can be made the night before and just warmed up in the morning. Overnight oats are also a great, quick breakfast. You could also have your yogurt, granola, and fruit set out for you so that you can just quickly eat it. Pancakes can also be made in advance and frozen, then you can just defrost them when you are ready to eat. There are plenty of good ideas for a make-ahead breakfast.

You should also pack your lunch the night before. That way, it is easy for you just to grab it and head to work. The best way to plan a meal for lunch is to make extra of what you made for dinner the night before. If you are making chicken for dinner, make some extra so that you can have a chicken salad, sandwich, or wrap the next day for lunch. This creates less work for you because you are basically killing two birds with one stone.

Dinners are usually the thing people struggle with the most. There are many options for what to make for dinner, and it is always good to try something different when you have the time. One of the best tips is to just have the base of your recipes ready so that you only have to do minimal cooking when you get home. Pick one day of the week where you prep all your food. Try and pick meals that have similar ingredients so that you can make things in batches.

Youan cut all your meat and vegetables on your meal prep day, so when you need them, you can just throw them in the pan or oven. If you can cook them on that day, it works even better. If you have made a whole bunch of chicken breast, you can add it to pasta, eat it with rice and veggies, or create a pulled chicken dish. Having a few things ready to go really helps you speed up the cooking process, and it allows you to have delicious things for dinner because it won't take up too much of your time.

HABIT 14: HAVE SOME TIME TO UNWIND

Rest is not something spoken about in today's hustle culture. People are always bragging about how much they work and how busy they are. We never hear about the rest that is needed. (Yeah, wouldn't it be nice if people didn't always respond to the question of "How are you?" with an answer of "Oh, I'm good, just really busy."?It may even sound a bit strange to have a section on resting when this book is about productivity and how to gain time and not waste it. Resting is not a waste of time when done appropriately. It can actually be the thing that allows you to be more productive.

We need to have a balanced life. If we never take time to rest and recharge, we will not have the energy to work to our full potential the next day. Naturally, we all get a bit tired towards the end of the day. This is our bodies telling us that we need to relax. All work and no rest leads to burnout, and that will cause you to waste weeks, even months. It is much better to take an hour or so to really relax at the end of the day rather than be forced to rest when you reach burnout.

Since rest is not glorified in society, many people are actually unsure how to do this effectively. We all know how to be lazy, but rest is something completely different. When we have a lazy day, we can end up feeling tired at the end of the day even though we didn't do anything. This is not proper rest. Knowing how to wind down, sleep well, and really rest is one of the best things you can learn to do for your physical and mental health. How to Unwind

Unwinding in the evening is a great habit to get into. It will help you relax and even sleep better. Unwinding will look different for everyone because every person has different likes and dislikes as well as things that help them relax. Much of this is trial and error, but, it will be much easier to learn how to relax properly if you know yourself.

The first thing you will need to do is to create a separation from work. If you are still thinking about work, then your mind will not be able to fully relax. You also have to cut off work. That means no looking at work emails or quickly switching on your laptop to check something. Once you decide that you are done with work, all things work-related must be left alone. For people who are very into their careers, this is the most challenging thing to do, but it is very important. If you receive your work emails on your phone, you will have to deactivate it or completely leave your phone alone for the rest of the evening.

Spending time with people you love is also a great way to unwind. You can spend time with your significant other or close friends. When we are engaging in conversation, our minds are present in the conversation rather than thinking about the things we have to get done. You can laugh, vent, share stories, and just enjoy the company of others. No matter how introverted someone is, good company is always needed and welcomed at the right time.

Meditating is a great way to clear your mind after a long day. Living in a fast-paced society means that our minds are always moving. Training our minds to slow down and stop for a few minutes is a valuable skill. One of the most common reasons people struggle to fall asleep is because their minds are racing. Knowing how to calm your mind will prevent this. Doing this well before you go to bed is even better.

Another way you can unwind is by doing something you enjoy. We hardly ever get the chance to do something fun or that we simply like doing. Dedicating a small portion of your day to a hobby or just doing something you enjoy increases your happiness and helps you feel more content. This doesn't have to be something big. Watching an episode of your favorite series, cooking, playing an instrument, doing yoga, going for a walk, and reading are amongst some of the options. If you have always wanted to get into something but never found the time, you can use a few minutes at the end of the day to dedicate to it.

How to Sleep Better

We can't speak about rest and not mention sleep. It is one of the most neglected needs that we have. The body needs to sleep for a certain amount of time and have that sleep be good quality. Not having a good night's sleep will definitely impact your productivity the next day. It is pretty sad that the first thing people give up when they are under pressure is their sleep. People often run on five to six hours of sleep a night. While it may seem like a good idea when you have a lot to get done, it is going to have negative impacts in the long run. When you have had a good sleep, you will wake up feeling energized, and your mind will be able to focus. This is the recipe for a successful and productive day. From this day forward, the challenge is for you to be intentional about your sleep.

Getting a good night's sleep is very much dependent on the things you do before you sleep. The hour before you jump into bed is the most essential part of your day where sleep is concerned. If you have followed the above tips, you will be in a good place come bedtime. When you unwind, you remove stress, which makes it easier for you to fall asleep. The goal is for you to fall asleep as quickly as possible from the time your head hits the pillow.

Ideally, you shouldn't be eating anything close to bedtime. We often confuse being hungry for being tired, so then we eat only to realize that we weren't that hungry. Being too full can cause us not to want to go to bed because we are slightly uncomfortable. It can also cause acid reflux when you try to lie down after you have eaten, which will make it even harder for you to fall asleep. Sugary foods and food that is high in caffeine should not be consumed at any point close to bedtime. In fact, you should cut these things off in the afternoon so that any stimulating effects wear off. When it comes to drinks that are high in caffeine, aim to have your last cup at about two in the afternoon. This will give the caffeine enough time to run its course through your body. You want to be able to relax when it gets close to bedtime, and if you eat or drink the wrong things, it will make it quite difficult to fall asleep when you want to.

Our bodies love routines, and we can use this to our advantage when it comes to sleep. Having a nightly routine is actually an excellent tool for falling asleep quickly. When you do the same few tasks every single night before you head off to bed, you will find that your body naturally starts getting sleepy. It's a great way to get yourself ready for bed and actually fall asleep when you crawl into bed.

It is important to pick tasks that are not strenuous and are pretty slow-paced. Taking a bath, brushing your teeth, reading a book, writing in a journal, setting out your clothes for the morning, and making a cup of caffeine-free tea are all great options. You can start your routine about 30 minutes before you get into bed. This will give you enough time to wind down slowly for bed. You should not be on your phone or any other device that emits blue light in these 30 minutes. The blue light will signal your body that it is daytime, and you will struggle to fall asleep. Instead set your alarm and answer any messages you need to before you start your bedtime routine.

Your bedroom should be a place of relaxation and calm. This is what will help you to fall asleep. If you usually do any work on your bed, then you should shift this and try and make your room a no-work zone. When you walk into your bedroom, you should feel like you want to relax and actually go to bed. You will find it difficult to sleep in the place you work, so it is not a good idea to mix the two. What constitutes a relaxing room will be different for everyone, but some basic concepts are a clean space, comfy bed, neutral colors, and free of loud noises. Play around with this until you are able to create a space that allows you to feel relaxed.

Some people have found great success with playing some soft, mellow music in the background while they are completing their nighttime routine. Dimming the lights is also a great option, especially if you have very harsh lighting in your room. Lamps with a slightly more orange tint are far better for bedrooms because they have a softer effect than bright white lights.

Doing all of this might seem a bit too much just to go to sleep, but it is worth it. You will see that it isn't as much work as it sounds when you start doing it. You will start looking forward to your winding-down time, and your sleep quality will improve. Both the length of your sleep and the quality of your sleep are important, so make sure you are paying attention to both.

HABIT 15: PLAN YOUR NEXT DAY

A great start to the morning begins the night before. Taking the time to plan out your day the night before can dramatically increase your productivity, not only in the mornings but throughout the entire day. Since this is not a stressful task, it can be added to your evening routine and your unwinding time. You are not attached to the next day as of yet, so all of your decisions will be objective and calm. We can get so caught up with everything we need to do in a day that we don't have a clear mind to plan the day with. When you plan the night before, it separates you from the stress of the day so that you can plan completely objectively.

When you plan your day the night before, you are reserving your decision-making energy for things that matter. This probably didn't make any sense when you first read it, but let me explain. Decision-making is drawn from our willpower. We make good decisions when our willpower is high and bad ones when it is low. Willpower is like an energy tank—as we go through the day, the tank drains out (Rao, 2020). Once we have used up our willpower for the day, we have to wait for it to be replenished the next day. If you think this is far-fetched, you should put it to the test. See how good your decision-making is in the morning compared to in the evening. You will find that you probably care a lot less in the evening. This is because you have a lower amount of willpower.

Our whole day is spent making decisions. We have to say no to certain things, decide what to eat, choose our clothes, make big decisions at work, and make a whole host of other choices. The more choices we make in the morning, the less we will be able to make throughout the day. This is why Steve Jobs wore the same outfit every single day; he didn't want to waste his willpower deciding what to wear. There are many other influential people that follow the same practices. They limit the number of choices they have to make in the morning so that they can be more productive throughout the day.

When you plan out your next day the night before, you eliminate many decisions from your morning. Don't get confused. Planning decisions for the next day does take a little bit of mental power, but it's easier to *plan* the decision than to *make* the decision. Think back to habit 3—preview your day. This habit will be much easier if you have done the planning the night before. You might have to make a few adjustments, but the bulk of the work will be done the night before. These two habits go hand in hand and work together to allow you to have a productive day. When you get into work, you can get through the game plan and dive into productive action faster! This also saves you a lot of time in the morning. You have already hashed out all the details so you can use your most productive time to actually work. Eliminating any extra work or tasks from your mornings is a great way to optimize your time since most people are the most productive earlier on in the day.

HABIT 16: POWER OF POSITIVITY

What you fill your mind with will determine how you act and your outlook on life. People who are always negative tend to limit themselves because they close themselves off to the opportunities that could be waiting just around the corner. Yes, life can be tricky sometimes, but there is always a silver lining. We just have to train ourselves to see the positives. We need to be pouring positivity into our own lives.

You may wonder why this habit is in a chapter about the end of a day. That is because if you have to have one more thing going through your mind before you head off to bed, it should be something positive. Positivity should flow through every area of your life. It will improve your mood and also calm your mind. If you are negative all the time, you will be stressed and worried because your mind will automatically go to the things that could go wrong. This is not a healthy space to be in. Besides, worst-case scenarios hardly ever happen. It is always better to think the best rather than to keep expecting the worst.

If you struggle with this, start off by preparing for the worst and hoping for the best. Regardless of how negative your mind can be, it can absolutely be rewired into a positive state. Including a dash of optimism into your mental preparation for the hardships of life not only increases your hopes, but when they actually come true from time to time, you will believe in them even more. While you are still preparing for the worst in this state of positive thinking, you also curb the shock of something terrible happening because you allow yourself to realize that bad things can happen, and you need to be prepared in case they do. This is quite a bit different than *expecting* bad things to happen, though, so don't mix those two ideas up.

Filling yourself with positivity might be something foreign to you, so you might not know how to implement this in your life. There are many ways to do this, and it might look different for everyone. If you are stuck and need some guidance, you can use some of the following ideas to help bring some positivity into your life. You can do these things at any point of the day, but they easily fit into your evening routine. This will help you get a peaceful night's sleep, and you will wake up in a better mood.

Keep a Gratitude Journal

Being grateful for the things in your life is one of the easiest ways to cultivate and maintain a positive mindset. Most of us have a much better life than we think we do. When we are going about our day, we don't stop and think about all the good that surrounds us. Workdays can be so hectic and packed with activities that we just don't stop for a little while to be thankful.

A gratitude journal helps make being thankful a daily habit. It forces us to stop and really think about the things we are grateful for. Even on the worst day, there will be something to be thankful for. If you had a tough day at work, at least you have a job to go to. If you had a falling out with a close friend, you could be thankful for the other people in your life that you have to lean on. Being grateful helps you to focus on the little things that are so easily missed in the day-to-day.

When we really think about it, we will find that there is a lot to be grateful for. We see that we have it much better than a lot of other people. This can help us appreciate what we have and even lead us to give back to those less fortunate. All of this can breed optimism for the future and allows us move into life with a better, more upbeat attitude. Intentionally opening our eyes to see the little things that help make our lives beautiful and fun helps us in more ways than we know.

Listen to Positive Affirmations

Sometimes we need an extra boost of positivity from an outside source, and we do this by hearing it. There are two ways you can do this. You can say the positive affirmations out loud, or you can listen to them. They both work really well, and which one you choose to go with is determined by personal preference.

Our minds will always register what we are listening to. This is why we get hurt by people's negative comments even though we try not to. It's also how our mood can suddenly improve by listening to happy music. We need to be conscious of what we are listening to, even when we aren't fully paying attention. We will still take in things, even if it is just background noise.

If you choose to say positive affirmations to yourself, you will be speaking and listening at the same time. These can also be tailored to what you are going through at the moment. You can use these affirmations to reassure yourself and help overcome any negative self-talk that may be going on. If you have a few statements saved, either in your mind or on a page in your notebook, you can be ready to say them whenever you need to. It is like having a positivity weapon in your arsenal.

You can also listen to prerecorded positive affirmations. These are great to listen to—pop your headphones into your ears and fill your mind! There are plenty of positive affirmations on public platforms like YouTube and music streaming services. You can also make your own by recording yourself and saving it. Listening to positive affirmations that have already been done for you might be an excellent place to start because it will give you guidance on the things you can be saying to yourself. You can also put a whole playlist of them on and let it run in the background while you are doing other tasks.

Listen to Something That Inspires You

Sometimes all we need to be a bit more positive is to be inspired. When we are inspired, we feel a sense of awe and wonder. It is very difficult to be in a negative space when you have all of these feelings and emotions going on. For inspiration, TED talks, podcasts, documentaries, and videos are all great to listen to or watch.

Clearly, there are a lot of options to intake this positive content. It does not only have to come from affirmations, but rather any source that can influence you in a good way. Positivity can be cultivated in several different ways, so naturally, we have to remember that negativity can as well. If you are going to use these mediums to listen to something that inspires you, you should also guard yourself against listening to anything negative. Most platforms have things that can fall into both the negative and positive columns. There is no need to be filling your mind with negative views and things that put you in a bad mental space. If you do find yourself consuming negative content, make a switch and look for something that is positive and inspiring.

Laugh Whenever You Can

Laughter is one of the most powerful yet underrated sources of positivity in the world. It can change your mood quickly and just make you feel good. People who laugh a lot are happier because laughter releases the feel-good hormone in your body. It is challenging to be in a bad mood or negative after you have had a good laugh. Because of this, you end up being more positive. Your mind just won't go to the negative side of things when you are having fun.

THE POSITIVITY POLICY

You can always find humor in things if you pay attention with an open mind. Most situations are not so serious that there can't be something funny to find in them. You will see that there are different types of people when things start to go wrong at an event. The first type is those that start stressing or get angry because things aren't going according to plan. The second type is the ones that take it in their stride and find humor in the situation. You will find that the latter will enjoy almost anything, and they are the type of people other people want to invite to things.

Life really isn't that serious, so find places that you can laugh. Look for the lighter side in everything because there is always one. Good stories come from things that did not go according to plan. If everything followed the script, then we would have nothing to talk about, and everything would just be boring. This is not the life that you should be aiming for. Look for moments where you can just crack a joke, or if someone else is making a joke, just go along with it. You will also attract more fun people to you if you are a fun and lighthearted person to be around.

You don't only have to find humor in real-life situations. You can also surround yourself with things that make you happy and make you laugh. There are plenty of series and movies out there that will really make a person laugh. You can watch one of those or watch a comedy skit of some sort. The point is that you can find a place to let loose and have a laugh. It is healthy for you, and you will find that you have a more positive outlook because you have laughed and enjoyed yourself.

Surround Yourself With Positive People

Positivity is contagious. It is also something that you should be cultivated throughout your day and your life as a whole. When you have the right people around you, you will feed off their energy. We tend to become like the people we spend the most time with, so it's vital to choose wisely, as we stated earlier on. Seriously, we cannot stress enough how much your friendship circle will impact both your outlook on life and your success.

The right friends hold you accountable and make sure that you are okay. They help you see life in a better way when you are having a bad day. Good friends won't let you wallow in a negative space for long. If you have friends that feed negativity, it is time to get some new friends. The truth is that you can't be the only positive one in a group of negative people. As much as you want to be the change, more often than not, you will be the one that they influence. Negativity is a very easy thing to catch if you don't cut it off soon enough. Pick the right friends, and you will find that your life is filled with quite a bit more happiness, and you are a much more positive person.

HABIT 17: PUT YOUR PHONE AWAY

We know that we have mentioned your phone quite a few times in this book. This is because our phone is something that we integrate into almost every single part of our day, and it is not doing us any favors. It is great to be connected to our friends and family, but if we are honest, most of the time we spend on our phones is wasted time. We don't have much to show for it, but we still find ourselves stuck to our phones for most of the day.

We wake up and scroll through our phones, and then we close out our days on our phones until we fall asleep. It is like an addiction that needs to be broken. Once you realize how much better you feel by limiting your phone time, you won't want to go back to the way you used to do things. If you struggle with falling asleep, then your phone is probably the most significant contributor to the problem. It could also be the reason you feel so tired even when you do sleep for a good number of hours.

When we take our phone to bed with us, we can sit up staring at it for hours, accomplishing nothing. Most of us are not just able to check social media and log off after five minutes. We just want to keep scrolling, watching, or reading. It is very difficult to stop once we have started. This is why so many people end up falling asleep with their phones in their hands. The only thing that can prevent them from falling asleep is literally being so exhausted that their body taps out. This is definitely not a healthy way to live, and this sort of thing spills over into other areas of our lives.

If you find that you are constantly on your phone in the morning and evening, there is a high chance that you are glued to it throughout the day as well. Sleep is not the only thing that suffers when you are always on your phone. We can get so caught up with what is on the screen that we forget to look up and experience the world around us. Staring at our screens for long periods of time forces us into a virtual world and makes us forget the real world without even realizing it.

Have you ever been out with someone and find yourself constantly checking your phone? What about having to ask someone to repeat themselves because you were too distracted to hear what they said? These are things that we have all done at some point, and it is a sign that we are addicted to our phones. Spending so much time on your phone is actually a waste of time because you are investing in something that is not going to give you a very good return.

If we don't make a conscious effort to put the phone away, we will never be able to build meaningful relationships. The truth is all those Instagram followers you have are not going to be there for you when you really need someone. Genuine relationships are built by having real, face-to-face connections with the people around you. Interacting and talking to people is something that we all need to make a priority because it builds our relationships and makes us feel better in the process. Healthy, strong relationships are something that is necessary in every person's life.

Make an effort to put your phone away when you are with other people. A great tip is to make dinner tables and family spaces a no-phone zone. This will allow everyone to connect with each other and have honest conversations. If you are going out with friends, you can ask everyone to put their phones in the middle of the table, and no one is allowed to touch them. You can even make it into a challenge. The first person to touch their phone has to buy the table a round of drinks! However you choose to implement this habit, the most important thing is that you do it. It will change your life and relationships in ways you will never know until you experience it.

It might be difficult to limit your screen time when you first start off. Phones have become so integrated into our lives that we don't even think about their impact. We include our phones in every part of our lives, mindlessly. Once you start putting up boundaries with your phone, you will be rewarded with more time to do things that you actually want to do and with richer relationships. You will find that you are less distracted, more present in the moment, and the resulting focus will help you accomplish the goals you've set in faster time frames.

6

GETTING TIME TAKES TIME

When it comes to changing your habits and taking on new habits, you should know that it will take some time. We all want to reap the rewards as soon as possible, but for some of the habits we've targeted, you will only get the full benefits after doing them consistently. There will definitely be a few immediate benefits, but consistency is key if you want to truly reap the productivity and time rewards throughout the course of your life.

There is a very common myth that it takes 21 days to form a new habit. Many people follow this and get lazy after 21 days because they think that the habit has been developed. The truth is that there is no magic number of days needed to create a habit. It is different for every person, and it also depends on the habit you are trying to create. If you are trying to develop the habit of drinking a glass of water every morning when you wake up, this new habit will take quicker than developing the habit of exercising for 30 minutes after work. It depends on how difficult the habit is to implement and how much willpower and effort it takes from your side. Rather than trying to reach a specific number of days, try and be as consistent as possible.

Another common reason people fail at building a habit is that they think they have to start from the beginning if they miss one day. There is no evidence to support the fact that missing a day or two has catastrophically negative impacts on habit formation. If you miss a day, just remember to do it the next day. One or two days does not ruin the process of habit formation, so don't stress out too much about it or be so strict on yourself that you lose motivation entirely. Since some habits can take a few months to actually become habits, it would be silly to think that one missed day is going to derail your progress altogether. Keep pushing, and eventually, it will take.

CHANGING YOUR BAD HABITS

Most of this book has been about building new habits, but it's essential to understand that these good habits will probably involve replacing some of your current habits that aren't so great. We all have them. If you ask the people you live with, I'm sure they have a list! Sometimes it becomes impossible to start a good habit if you have a bad habit in the same area. Breaking bad habits will not only help you create good habits, but it will be better for you overall.

We all inherently know our bad habits. Most of us have tried to break them at some point. The thing to note about breaking bad habits is it can feel like it's even more difficult than building new ones. This depends on the habit you are trying to break and how often you do it. It's like trying to clean up a mess; it is much more difficult than actually making the mess. Reversing bad habits takes more effort because you are trying to fix something and change behaviors that are probably ingrained in you.

Every habit has a root cause. In order to change it, you must identify the cause of it. If you have the habit of overeating, maybe it is a result of stress. If you scroll on your phone for hours, that might be a habit caused by trying to avoid awkward social situations. If you have the habit of always being late, then that could be caused by not planning well enough in advance. As you can see with these examples, you will need to deal with the root cause before you can fix the habit.

When dealing with the root cause of a habit, you could either try and replace it with another habit or remove the trigger. For example, if you overeat when you get stressed, you could try and replace eating with something else when you feel stressed. This might be chewing gum, drinking water, making a cup of tea, or going for a walk. This will allow you to do something healthier when you feel stressed. The other thing you could do is remove the sources of stress in your life. If seeing a certain person stresses you out or watching the news gives you that feeling, then try not to put yourself in those situations. It is much more difficult to remove the trigger in most cases because you aren't always in control of that. Controlling the way you react to certain things is a strategy that works for most people.

When you are trying to break a bad habit, you have to make a commitment to yourself that you will do it—a commitment that is accompanied by a time frame gives you something to work towards. You can say, "I am going to replace my habit of snacking on unhealthy food with eating fruit, and I will do it for one month." Giving yourself a goal to reach will provide you with something to work towards. You won't actually know if that habit will take a month to break, but you will be much closer at that point than you are now. Once you get there, you can reward yourself and then set another challenge for yourself. Don't go in with the expectation that you will break the habit in the specified time frame; instead, just set yourself the goal.

Accountability is also something that can really help you break your habit. Having someone who is able to check up on you makes it far more likely for you to succeed in what you do. Even if they don't check up on you at all, just telling someone about your plan to break or change your habits will make you more likely to do it. The reason for this is that we don't want to disappoint other people, and we don't want to embarrass ourselves by not completing the tasks that we said we would. As humans, we fear disappointing others far more than letting ourselves down. Now you don't have to go and tell every person that will listen. Pick one or two people who you know will be there for you and who will make the commitment to keeping you accountable. You can even work with someone else and share your progress. If you and your friend are both trying to break bad habits, you can do it together, even if their habit is different from yours. Using these mentalities and everything to follow within this chapter, along with having targeted the specific habits we've supplied throughout this book, will put you well on your way to mastering your time management skills and having more time daily to put toward things that matter the most in your life.

TIPS FOR MAKING YOUR HABITS STICK

Building a new habit does take work and commitment, but once it has stuck, it takes a lot less work to keep going. You will be following through automatically without much effort from your side. We know it is going to take consistency, but there are a few other things that you can do to make sure that you build and keep good habits.

Start Small and Build Up

When you start a new habit, you should always start small. If you decided you wanted to work out every single day and jumped in to do two-hour sessions every single afternoon, it wouldn't last too long. We need to get used to the change before we can even think about going all in. Jumping straight in is unsustainable because the drastic change is going to be difficult and could cause a loss of motivation. If someone who has never gone to the gym before did a two-hour session, they would be so sore the next day that they would never want to exercise again. The goal of a habit is for it to be sustainable, so if you can see a particular practice is not something you can follow, you will need to adjust it.

The better approach is to think a tad smaller, such as going for a 15-minute walk every day. This is a light form of exercise, and it is something that can be squeezed into your day. Eventually, you can increase this to 30-minute walks and then one-hour walks. Slowly, you can switch to something that is a little more challenging. You can do a light gym session or start a kickboxing class. It won't be a far stretch because you have already carved out time to walk every day, so all you are doing is replacing the walking with something else. The main thing would be getting into the habit of doing something. It is easier to replace a particular practice with something else than to build up a new habit from scratch.

This principle works for every other habit you might want to form. If you're going to start reading every day, start by reading one page and build from there. If you want to wake up earlier, start by waking up 10 minutes earlier instead of a full hour earlier. One word of caution here is that once you reach your end goal, stop pushing yourself. It would be a bit ridiculous to keep trying to wake up 10 minutes earlier when you already wake up at 5 a.m. There is a point where you will just have to maintain the habit rather than build upon it, so keep that in mind as you are trying to add on a bit more to your habits.

Do It One at a Time

We spoke about 17 habits to build in order to master your time management skills, but it would be pretty impossible to do them all at once. You could definitely try, but they will not stick because too many aspects of your life would be variable, and they will all take mental and physical effort to maintain consistency. Each of them takes time to become automatic, so every one of the 17 would be manually forced to happen at once, which is exceptionally challenging. Very soon, you will more than likely give up or break down with a loss of motivation. Building one habit is hard, so trying to do 17 all at once is a recipe for disaster.

It is best to pick one (or a few if you can manage it) and really focus on building it well and in a sustainable manner. If you decide to do more than one, make sure that they fall in the same category, and you are able to flow from one to another easily. For example, if you choose to build the habit of waking up earlier, then you can also build the habit of reading in the morning or doing some exercise. This makes sense because you will need to do something to fill that time if you wake up earlier. You can use this to your advantage and try to squeeze in another good habit into your day.

Pick the habit that you think would add the most value to your life at this point. Only you will know what to choose because you know yourself better than anyone else. You also know your bad habits, so you can choose to build a good habit that can counteract the bad ones that you have. If you are having trouble and need the input of a mentor, start by asking them to help point out a bad habit to begin with. It can be more challenging to be honest with ourselves when it comes to our bad habits, and establishing which is the most relevant right now will also help guide you to which good habit to pick to replace it with. As a word of caution, choose the person whose opinion you invite very carefully, and also prepare yourself to gather some honest input from them, so your feelings don't get hurt in the process. Sometimes replacing a bad habit with a good one is the easiest way to break the habit, and it is a way to kill two birds with one stone.

Set a Reminder

We are all humans, which means the chance that we will forget to do something is pretty high. Habits are formed by being consistent, but if something is completely new to us, it will be easy to forget to do that thing. Let's use the example of planning out your day the night before. If this is the habit that you are trying to form, but you have never done it before, you will probably forget to sit down and do it every night. It is easy to get caught up in your old evening routine and let this slip your mind.

There are plenty of ways you can remind yourself to do this task. You could set a reminder on your phone. Set it to ring about ten minutes before you want to do the tasks so that you remember to do them. If you are trying to avoid your phone in the evenings, then you can set non-digital reminders. Sticky notes work great, so write down your reminder and place it somewhere you know you will see it. If you brush your teeth every night before bed, then you can stick the reminder on your bathroom mirror. You could also remind yourself by using prompts. You could place your notebook and pen on your pillow or on your bedside table so that you see them when you are getting ready for bed.

Reminding yourself of the habits you are trying to form will help you to stick to the process. We can't always trust our brains to remember what we have to do, especially if we have a default that is not in line with the habit we are trying to build.

Remove the Temptation

When you are trying to create a new habit or even break an old one, you have to consider that it is changing thought and action patterns. Something that has been fine for you to do for a long time will suddenly not be okay. Introducing a new habit into your life means that you will have to make some shifts in other areas to accommodate this change. This may not be easy, so you don't want to make it harder for yourself.

If a temptation can derail the habit you are trying to build, you should remove that thing as much as possible. If you are starting a habit to eat healthier, it will not help to have a cupboard filled with chocolate and candy. If you remove all of this junk food, there will be fewer temptations and a higher chance of you sticking to your habit.

This principle can work for any habit. If you are trying to quit social media, then delete the apps. If you are trying to wake up earlier, remove the things that keep you up, like TV shows, social media, and your phone. If you are trying to build a habit of getting into deep work, you will have to remove distractions. As much as it is possible for you to do so, remove temptations and things that can possibly derail your progress.

Get Inspired

It can be difficult to stick to a plan or mindset if you feel that you don't have support or that you are the only one in it. Listening to other peoples' stories or to motivational speakers will empower you with that extra bit of inspiration to keep going and find new ways of doing things. Following people that have already been where you have been or are interested in the same things as you can really give you a boost.

You can find people to follow and watch on any social media platform. Many people who have lots of followers and are social media influencers in some capacity create communities of like-minded people. If someone is a fitness influencer, the people that follow them will be into that type of content. If you want to get fitter, you should follow pages and channels of people like this. You can learn so much from their stories, and in the comment sections, people can also help guide and give you advice when you need it.

There is so much content out there, so you are bound to find something that will be up your alley. The more you surround yourself with the stories and content of those with similar goals to you or have already reached those goals, the more inspired you will get. It helps to hear how other people do things and how they overcome their challenges. It will reassure you that you can do it too and give you different ideas and perspectives when you need them.

Keep Track

Building habits is about consistency, but it is difficult to know how far you have come unless you keep track of it. It is easy to feel stuck in the place you are if you feel like you are not making progress. We shouldn't trust our minds to keep track of how far we have come. It gets used to where you are now, and you won't be able to see a big difference. If you live with a child who is in their teens or pre-teens, you have probably heard people comment about how much they have grown. You probably did not notice it that much because you see the child every single day. If you kept track of the child's height, you would have been able to see the progress. The same thing happens to us and anything in our lives. We have to track in order to see the difference.

By tracking your habits, you will be able to tell how far you have come, but it will also show you periods where you have not improved, or you have gone backward. It doesn't have to be a huge mission to track your habits. There are many apps out there that do this for you— all you have to do is input the relevant information. An even more straightforward way of tracking your habits is to use a calendar. If you completed the habit on a certain day, then mark it with an X on the calendar. You will be able to see how many consecutive days you have kept your habit.

Many people use the method above to help motivate them to keep the habit going. It is called the *don't break the chain* method. The longer your chain of Xs on the calendar, the more you want to keep going. It is a challenge to see how long you can keep the chain going by completing your habits. You will find that having this visual representation of your progress will keep you more motivated. You can also create checkpoints with rewards once you get there. This is another way to add some motivation to your habit building.

Allow Yourself to Have Bad Days

There will be some days where you will have to skip out on trying to form new habits. Life can be unpredictable, and sometimes it is just not possible to keep something up every single day. This does not mean that you shouldn't try your best to keep it going, but if there is a day that you miss, you should give yourself grace for this.

If you push too hard, you will make yourself sick of the process. It is entirely okay to miss a day because of something unexpected or simply because you do not feel like it. The important thing is that you get back on track as soon as possible. A great rule to follow is the two-day rule. You should never break your habit for two days in a row. If you skip one day, then the next day, make it a non-negotiable goal to get it done. This prevents you from falling off the bus, but it also gives you some flexibility when you need it. In most cases, you will be able to get back on track after missing out on the habit once.

Just Do Something

Most people don't follow through with their habit-forming practices because they feel it gets to be too much on certain days. When it comes to habits, it is vital to do something every day. This does not mean that you have to do the whole habit, just something so that you can keep yourself on track. If you are working on an exercise habit, but one of the days you don't feel like exercising, instead of forcing yourself to exercise or skipping it altogether, do a quick two-minute workout or a five-minute walk.

Just doing something allows you to keep the momentum even though you are not completing the full habit. Sometimes it is just about keeping the rhythm rather than keeping the same level of effort. The hardest thing about developing a new habit is the fact that you have to integrate it into your schedule. So if a five-minute walk is the only thing that fits into your schedule on a specific day, then you should do it. Doing something is always better than doing nothing.

It's About Lifestyle

With the habits you're seeking to learn about, implement, and master in this book, it is more about creating a new lifestyle through several small changes than just implementing a few habits. When the word habit is mentioned, people often just think that you can put your body on autopilot, and it will do what it needs to do if you have created the right habits. This is simply not true. Some habits can be done without thinking about them, but these are usually the smaller habits. Brushing your teeth, the way you greet the people around you and perhaps having a cup of coffee in the morning are all habits if you do them regularly. These habits are ones that are incredibly easy to do because they do not require much brainpower, and you can do them without much resistance from other areas of your life.

When it comes to more significant habits, you have to put in more effort, and this effort cannot just evaporate completely once the habit is formed. Once the habit is solid in your routine, it will be easier to do it, and you will find yourself gravitating towards doing it. However, that does not mean that it will be utterly devoid of attention on your part. It is easy to pick up the phone in the evening, even when you have made it a habit to put it away before bed. You could want to sleep in on a specific day, even though you have worked hard to form the habit of waking up early. These are all very normal things that can happen, and it's important to mentally accept the fact that they will still take some effort and energy from time to time to keep from losing their level of effectiveness.

The good news is that if you mess up your habit, it will be easier to get back on track. Muscle memory is just as effective with your brain because you know it is a muscle. Once you recognize that you're slipping, just give yourself a push in the right direction to revamp that particular habit. With the bigger ones, it is essential to know that you are building a lifestyle and not just making a bunch of random habits. This is why we suggested that you pick the habits that fit you, your needs, and your lifestyle, so all of the core habits work together to help you with the life you are building.

Be Aware of Your Excuses

We have spoken about not sweating it if you have missed a day or two when trying to build a habit. However, it is important to know your common excuses so that you can look out for them. We will often say we can't do something and give a real reason, but if we were to dig a little deeper, we would see that we really just don't feel like inconveniencing ourselves at that moment. The reasoning we have given is just an excuse because we are too lazy or are not in the mood.

If we know what our excuses are, we will be able to catch ourselves in the act. You need to ask yourself, "What is getting in the way of this habit?" Really think about all the things that you use as an excuse to skip it for a day. You will most likely find that these things can be easily solved. You can then put things in place so that you can't use that as an excuse any longer. This will help you to push through and form the habits even when you really don't want to.

We did say earlier to give yourself grace, but if you find yourself making it a habit of constantly forgiving yourself, you're probably not gaining any ground on the progress you're aiming to create. For example, if you went to your best friend's wedding and stayed up late celebrating, letting yourself sleep in for a few extra hours the next day is not unrealistic. On the contrary, if you want to sleep in on Thursday because it's rainy and you're cozy in your bed, that's a little different scenario. You have to be able to recognize when you're giving yourself excuses compared to unique and uncommon events.

Create a Routine

We are far more likely to do something if we have set a time and a place for it. When it becomes a routine in our lives, then we just do it because we are used to it. It has a designated space, so we make sure it gets done. When we just say we are going to do something, it is too up in the air for us to be sure that we will actually stick to it. We are more likely to stick to things that have a designated area in our lives than just something that is on a to-do list.

Take habit 13, for example. You want to plan your meals and prep for the week, so you decide you are going to tackle that. If you do not put down a set time and date to do it, it will never get done. When we do not have things set in stone for us, we go according to our feelings. We will do things when we feel like doing them. The problem is that we don't often feel like doing hard things, so those things will never get done. These things don't have to be tough things to do, but even if they are slightly inconvenient, we can easily choose not to do them at the moment if we do not have it scheduled. This is why making commitments to yourself and writing them down is so important.

Just Enjoy the Process

While building a new habit might be a bit difficult, it is also a really great experience. You get to discover new things about yourself and learn new disciplines. As much as we might not like to admit it, learning is something that most humans enjoy to some degree. We like discovering something new about ourselves and giving ourselves a challenge. Humans weren't meant to always be comfortable. We were meant to take up challenges and constantly change. Staying the same is boring, so you realize that you will want to create these new habits because it betters you.

It can be a gratifying process if you want it to be. People who drag their feet and complain when they have to do something new are the types of people who choose to put a ceiling on their lives. You will only be able to grow according to the level that you allow yourself to change and grow. You are the most limiting factor in your own life, so that means that you are the only one that has the power to change that. Imagine being the same person you were when you were a teenager. We can all agree that we are thankful we grew out of that stage. Those ideas and mindsets would not have been able to carry us through life and get us to where we are now. The same can be said for every stage of life. There is always room to learn, grow, and change.

If you are not the type of person that likes learning and improving, then it will be very difficult to make the right changes in your life. Allowing yourself to enjoy the process means that you will want to keep growing and changing. If there is another habit that you want to implement, you will be motivated to do so. If you feel naturally opposed to growth, we would suggest sitting down and figuring out why. This way, you can deal with the problem so that it does not limit you. Once you really give yourself over to the process of learning, growing, and changing, it becomes something really enjoyable, and you will want to be present in the moment.

CONCLUSION

Now you know the 17 habits that are the keys to productivity and creating more time for yourself. These habits will carry you throughout every stage of life and help you maximize your experiences in each of those stages. Each one of them holds its own set of benefits, and they work together to create a lifestyle that can truly change the quality of the life you live. It is incredible what you can achieve and how much your day-to-day life can change by making some small changes.

Most people aren't conscious about their habits or their routines. This is limiting both in the short term and in the long run because you don't know the things that are holding you back. Most of life is not about making huge decisions or changes, but rather most of life is just the little things. It is taking every chance you get to improve.

CONCLUSION

The tips and principles that you have learned in this book will propel you in ways that you could previously only imagine, but only if you implement them well. The key to all success is not just knowing what you should do but actually implementing that knowledge into your own life. Half of the work is done because you know exactly what you have to do. The rest is up to you.

We are confident that you are inspired to make some changes in the way you do things. Just make sure that you make these changes in a sustainable way. Trying to change everything about the way you do things is unsustainable—if you try and do it all at once. Remember that you are going to be changing patterns and habits that have ingrained themselves in your life over many years. They can't be changed over the course of a few weeks. Slow and sustainable change is the way to go. You want this to be a lifestyle change and not just something you tried once upon a time.

If you are really intentional about applying these habits in your life, we have no doubt that you will see an increase in productivity, and you will be able to finish tasks quicker than before. There's no better feeling than knowing that you are putting in the work to reach your full potential and that in turn you will be able to reach your goals. There will be no more wasting your days and having to work late to finish work that could have been done during the day. This is the start of a much healthier and more well-balanced life for you.

CONCLUSION

When you implement these habits into your life, you are making a choice to improve your entire lifestyle. Diving in and really striving to master time management and your daily habits will lead you toward being able to spend time doing the things that you truly value in life with the people that matter the most to you. We often put the things that we love doing on the back burner because we don't have the time to do them, but that does not have to be an excuse anymore! Not only that but now that you are more productive with the time you get, you'll be prepared to squeeze as much as you can out of every second you've earned. Stop wishing or waiting for it to happen magically. You now know the habits that will give you the gift of time. All that's left to do is to go out and get it!

LEAVE A REVIEW

Being an independent author duo with a smaller marketing budget to spend, reviews make a world of difference in our success.

If you gained value from this book (or simply enjoyed it), we would be highly grateful if you leave your honest feedback in the form of a review where you purchased it.

We love hearing from our readers and personally read every review and take that feedback seriously. Your voice matters to us, so please share it!

WWW.POSITIVITYPOLICY.INFO

The practical checklist of
33 Stupid-Simple Negative Habits
and effortless suggestions to overcome

WWW.POSITIVITYPOLICY.NET

FREE GIFT FOR OUR READERS

Get a jump on eliminating negative habits and building your confidence with this checklist. Visit the link:

www.PositivityPolicy.info

REFERENCES

A.Linderstam, R. (2020, May 11). *Time manage like Elon Musk. A quick introduction to "timeboxing".* Medium. https://medium.com/@ralflinderstam/time-manage-like-elon-musk-a-quick-introduction-to-timeboxing-a4e874109519

Akhtar, A. (2019, April 22). *10 smartphone habits that are getting in the way of your success.* BusinessInsider. https://www.businessinsider.co.za/smartphone-habits-that-are-ruining-your-productivity-2018-7?r=US&IR=T#:~:text=For%20instance%2C%20overusing%20your%20phone

Boksic, B. (2013, May 13). *11 important things to remember when changing habits.* Lifehack. https://www.lifehack.org/articles/productivity/the-secret-changing-habits-successfully.html

REFERENCES

Clear, J. (n.d.-a). *The only productivity tip you'll ever need.* James Clear. https://jamesclear.com/productivity-tip#:~:text=Productivity%20is%20getting%20important%20things%20done%20consistently.&text=Being%20productive%20is%20about%20maintaining

Clear, J. (n.d.-b). *The value of time: How much is your time really worth?* James Clear. https://jamesclear.com/value-of-time

Clear, J. (2013, June 6). *How to stop procrastinating by using the "2-minute rule."* Lifehack. https://www.lifehack.org/articles/productivity/how-stop-procrastinating-and-stick-good-habits-using-the-2-minute-rule.html

Clear, J. (2018, July 13). *How long does it actually take to form a new habit? (Backed by science).* James Clear. https://jamesclear.com/new-habit

Clear, J. (2019, February 1). *How the 2-minute rule can help you beat procrastination and start new habits.* CNBC. https://www.cnbc.com/2019/02/01/the-2-minute-rule-how-to-stop-procrastinating-and-start-new-habits.html

Cooper, B. B. (2018, February 28). *Daily routines and schedules of 7 famous entrepreneurs.* Buffer Resources. https://buffer.com/resources/daily-schedule/

REFERENCES

Develop Good Habits. (2020, July 24). *11 ways to stay focused on your goals and avoid distractions.* Develop Good Habits. https://www.developgoodhabits.com/focus-goals/

Garfield, L. (2016, May 25). *Checking your phone first thing in the morning could be making you unhappy.* Business Insider. https://www.businessinsider.com/why-you-shouldnt-check-your-phone-first-thing-in-the-morning-2016-5?IR=T

Good Therapy. (2009, September 15). *Positive psychology.* Good Therapy. https://www.goodtherapy.org/learn-about-therapy/types/positive-psychology

Haas, S. B. (2018, April 17). *6 ways that night-time phone use destroys your sleep.* Psychology Today. https://www.psychologytoday.com/us/blog/prescriptions-life/201804/6-ways-night-time-phone-use-destroys-your-sleep

Hartwell-Walker, M. (2016, May 17). *7 steps to changing a bad habit.* Psych Central. https://psychcentral.com/lib/7-steps-to-changing-a-bad-habit#1

Just Energy. (n.d.). *How meal prepping saves you time, money, and energy.* Just Energy. https://justenergy.com/blog/how-meal-prepping-saves-you-time-money-and-energy/

Mayo Clinic. (2017). *How to stop negative self-talk.* Mayo Clinic; https://www.mayoclinic.org/healthy-lifestyle/stress-management/in-depth/positive-thinking/art-20043950

REFERENCES

Mindtools. (2019). *Timeboxing: Maximizing your productivity*. Mindtools. https://www.mindtools.com/pages/article/timeboxing.htm

Minimalism Made Simple. (2020, June 18). *15 truths about the value of time*. Minimalism Made Simple. https://www.minimalismmadesimple.com/home/the-value-of-time/

Minutillo, M. (2019, July 19). *There is always more to learn*. Medium. https://medium.com/swlh/there-is-always-more-to-learn-d549432da5e8

Nawalkha, A. (2018, May 10). *Master the art of decision making [10 secrets]*. Evercoach - by Mindvalley. https://www.evercoach.com/blog/10-secrets-that-will-help-you-master-the-art-of-decision-making

Nour Luxury. (2018, April 5). *How to relax before bed: Tips to help you unwind*. Nour Luxury. https://www.nourluxury.com/blogs/news/how-to-relax-before-bed#:~:text=Unwinding%20ensures%20a%20great%20night

Peters, B. (2020, May 20). *Why you should not sleep with your cell phone at night*. Verywell Health. https://www.verywellhealth.com/reasons-why-you-should-not-sleep-with-your-cell-phone-4140997#:~:text=If%20y-ou%20have%20already%20fallen

Pettit, M. (2018, August 28). *Why successful people take notes and how to make it your habit*. Lifehack. https://www.

REFERENCES

lifehack.org/796333/take-notes#:~:text=The%20art%20of%20note%20taking

Piedmont Healthcare. (n.d.). *5 benefits of morning exercise.* Piedmont Healthcare. https://www.piedmont.org/living-better/5-benefits-of-morning-exercise

Positive Creators. (2020, June 26). *7 benefits of listening to positive affirmations.* Positive Creators. https://positivecreators.com/7-benefits-of-listening-to-positive-affirmations/

Prince, R. (2021, March 21). *Is your smartphone ruining your sleep?* Sleep.org. https://www.sleep.org/is-your-smartphone-ruining-your-sleep/

Ramsey Solutions. (2021, March 9). *How to meal plan to save time and money.* Ramsey Solutions. https://www.ramseysolutions.com/budgeting/create-a-meal-plan

Rao, S. (2020, June 11). *Why planning your day the night before drastically increases your productivity.* Medium. https://medium.com/the-mission/why-planning-your-day-the-night-before-drastically-increases-your-productivity-a5b5d39ff2bb

Roomer, J. (2019, June 10). *12 empowering morning routine habits to prime yourself for A highly productive & successful day.* Medium. https://medium.com/personal-growth-lab/12-empowering-morning-routine-habits-to-prime-yourself-for-a-highly-productive-successful-day-885b89ebeadf

Roth, A. (2011, June 28). *Financial wealth - it's time not money.* CBS News. https://www.cbsnews.com/news/financial-wealth-its-time-not-money/

Rothman, J. (2019, January 14). *The art of decision-making.* The New Yorker. https://www.newyorker.com/magazine/2019/01/21/the-art-of-decision-making

Ruben, G. (2009, October 21). *Stop expecting to change your habit in 21 days.* Psychology Today. https://www.psychologytoday.com/us/blog/the-happiness-project/200910/stop-expecting-change-your-habit-in-21-days

Sanborn, M. (2017, September 15). *Think you've reached the top? There's always a way to improve.* Entrepreneur. https://www.entrepreneur.com/article/300360

Sisson, M. (2014, June 2). *7 nighttime rituals to help you unwind, relax, and chill out (that don't involve alcohol).* HuffPost. https://www.huffpost.com/entry/nighttime-rituals_b_5432187

Smith, C. (2018, October 23). *How to turn complex into simple.* Thinkbda.com. https://www.thinkbda.com/blog/how-to-turn-complex-into-simple

Still, J. (2019, May 9). *5 reasons to wake up early, even if you hate it.* Business Insider. https://www.businessinsider.com/

REFERENCES

reasons-to-wake-up-early-2019-5?IR=T#it-will-be-easier-to-stay-upbeat-3

Tejada, C. (2019, December 12). *Why your phone shouldn't be a part of your morning routine.* HuffPost Canada. https://www.huffingtonpost.ca/entry/dont-check-phone-in-morning_ca_5df24c1ae4b01e0f295b6d0a

The Sleep Advisor. (2020, June 8). *Benefits of waking up early - our 9 tips for making a morning routine.* The Sleep Advisor. https://www.sleepadvisor.org/benefits-of-waking-up-early/

The Wealth Advisor. (2019, October 22). *Elon musk's "time blocking" method: How to manage time effectively even if your schedule is hectic.* The Wealth Advisor. https://www.thewealthadvisor.com/article/elon-musks-time-blocking-method-how-manage-time-effectively-even-if-your-schedule-hectic

Todoist. (n.d.). *The complete guide to time blocking.* Todoist. https://todoist.com/productivity-methods/time-blocking

Umoh, R. (2018, June 21). *Skyrocket your productivity with the "touch it once" rule.* CNBC. https://www.cnbc.com/2018/06/21/touch-it-once-method-for-tasks-can-boost-productivity.html

Whalen, R. (2017, December 14). *6 amazing benefits of morning exercise.* Total Wellness. https://info.

REFERENCES

totalwellnesshealth.com/blog/6-amazing-benefits-of-morning-exercise

Young, S. H. (2007, August 14). *18 tricks to make new habits stick*. Lifehack; Lifehack. https://www.lifehack.org/articles/featured/18-tricks-to-make-new-habits-stick.html

ZME Science. (2017, April 5). *Why it's important to wind down before you go to bed*. ZME Science. https://www.zmescience.com/medicine/importance-relaxing-before-sleep/

ABOUT THE AUTHORS

We are The Positivity Policy! Our names are Kara and Denny, and one of our goals in life is to spread as much positivity and influence the world in the best way we know how; sharing what we've learned through our experiences!

Having both been through a ton of ups and downs through life, we are not claiming to know everything or are able to fix every problem. Rather, we want to offer a positive perspective to real-life situations and challenges that we've invested much time into learning how to process, approach, and overcome. Our life is one big fun adventure filled with raising three amazing boys, traveling and experiencing as much of the world as we can, and never skipping a chance to make memories with those we love. So if you want to be a part of our pursuit of positivity, grab one of our books, check out our blog at www.positivitypolicy.net, or join our Facebook tribe, The Positivity Policy!

www.ingramcontent.com/pod-product-compliance
Lightning Source LLC
Chambersburg PA
CBHW031423210526
45464CB00005B/2024